D0122103

Quiet Moments in the Presence of God

PRESENTED TO:

_____

PRESENTED BY:

_____

DATE:

_____

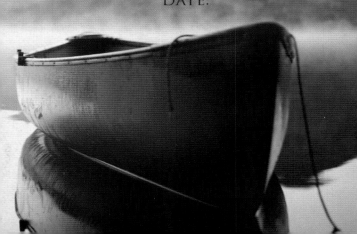

QUIET
MOMENTS
in the
PRESENCE
of GOD

QUIET
MOMENTS
in the
PRESENCE
of GOD

BETHANYHOUSE
MINNEAPOLIS, MINNESOTA

Quiet Moments in the Presence of God
Copyright © 2005 by GRQ Ink, Inc.
Brentwood, Tennessee 37027

Published by Bethany House Publishers
11400 Hampshire Avenue South
Bloomington, Minnesota 55438

Bethany House Publishers is a division of Baker Publishing Group, Grand Rapids, Michigan.

ISBN-13: 978-0-7642-0125-7   ISBN-10: 0-7642-0125-5

Editor: Lila Empson
Associate Editor: Natasha Sperling
Writer: Phillip H. Barnhart
Design: Whisner Design Group, Tulsa, Oklahoma

06 07 08 5 4 3

Say a quiet yes to God and he'll be there in no time.

JAMES 4:8 THE MESSAGE

CONTENTS

INTRODUCTION

There is no better place to be than in the presence of God. There is no better way to be in  the presence of God than to get quiet and to focus on God's love for and commitment to you. Focus your heart on God's passion, your mind on God's insight, and your will on God's plan and purpose for your life.

Quiet your body as you sit still; hush the nudge to be somewhere else.

Quiet your mind as you shake off the pressures of agenda and schedule.

Quiet your heart as you make God's presence your priority and relegate anything else to lesser importance.

This book invites you to turn up the quiet in your life, to be still and know God immediately and intimately.

G OD, my shepherd! I don't
need a thing. You have bed-
ded me down in lush mead-
ows, you find me quiet pools
to drink from.

Psalm 23:1–2 THE MESSAGE

You're my place of quiet
retreat; I wait for your
Word to renew me.

<small>PSALM 119:114 THE MESSAGE</small>

BE QUIET

They were glad because they had quiet, and he brought them to their desired haven.

PSALM 107:30 NRSV

The less busyness around you, the more you can feel the presence of God. The less you are aware of the noise of the world, the more you will understand the love of God. The less you listen to the unimportant and the non-essential, the more you will sense intimations and indications of God's presence.

Fill up the space between you and God with a silence that waits for God, acknowledges his great love for you, and anticipates that he is with you. If anything can go without saying, let it go. An absence of spoken words brings the quiet that makes possible the awed awareness of God.

Create in your environment and within your heart a chapel-hush that makes of your soul a sanctuary for the presence of God.

Paul stood on the stairs and motioned to the people to be quiet. Soon a deep silence enveloped the crowd, and he addressed them in their own language.

ACTS 21:40 NLT

When I am quiet, O God, I can hear you thinking your thoughts in my mind and making your way known in my heart. Amen.

GOD IS NEAR

Your GOD is present among you, a strong Warrior there to save you. Happy to have you back, he'll calm you with his love and delight you with his songs.

ZEPHANIAH 3:17 THE MESSAGE

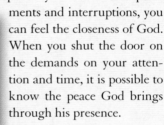

When you separate yourself from impediments and interruptions, you can feel the closeness of God. When you shut the door on the demands on your attention and time, it is possible to know the peace God brings through his presence.

A guide was directing visitors through a large city in his country, speaking to them in hesitant and halting English. As they went down one of the busiest streets in the city, he said to them in an urgent tone, "Stick on me." In moments of sacred quiet, you can get so close to God that your heart sticks to his.

When you separate yourself from what comes next on the list of things to do, you can move God to the top of the list of places to be.

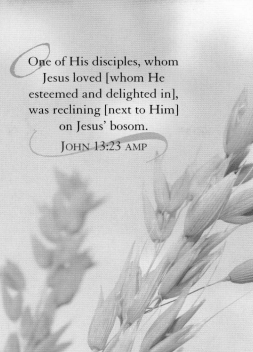

One of His disciples, whom
Jesus loved [whom He
esteemed and delighted in],
was reclining [next to Him]
on Jesus' bosom.

JOHN 13:23 AMP

When I quiet my soul,
O God, you are nearer than
breathing—closer to me than
I am to myself.

Amen.

A SPECIFIC SALUTATION

This, then, is how you should pray: "Our Father in heaven: May your holy name be honored; may your Kingdom come; may your will be done on earth as it is in heaven."

MATTHEW 6:9–10 GNT

The disciples saw Jesus often on bended knee and, one day, asked him to teach them how to pray. He taught them that the first thing to do is to address God directly, to be specific in salutation, to know what God means, and to call him what he is.

Prayer acknowledges the personal nature of your relationship to God. God is a friend with whom you share and in whom you confide. Through prayer, you speak to God and God speaks to you. The strength of your prayer comes from the intensity of your bond with God.

When you talk to God, you talk to someone you know well and with whom you have a deep and close relationship.

God! Let people thank and enjoy you. Let all people thank and enjoy you.

PSALM 67:3 THE MESSAGE

Dear God of heaven and earth, I am first to you and you are foremost to me.

Amen.

SIT IN SILENCE

For God alone my soul waits in silence, from him comes my salvation. He alone is my rock and my salvation, my fortress; I shall never be shaken.

PSALM 62:1–2 NRSV

Silence is golden when you desire God's presence. It closes down the racket made by  urgent schedule and full agenda. With those noises dismissed, you have a clear channel. Silence enables you to hear with your heart as God speaks from his.

Sitting in silence in a quiet place gives God a chance to bless you. In the only one of Phillips Brooks's hymns to survive the test of time, "O Little Town of Bethlehem," a line in the third stanza reads, "How silently, how silently, the wondrous gift is given!" As you wait and watch in silence, God touches you with the blessing of his presence.

Silence beckons you into intimacy with God. God's best gift, the gift of himself, is often given in silence.

When the Lamb broke open
the seventh seal, there was
silence in heaven for about
half an hour. Then I saw the
seven angels who stand
before God, and they were
given seven trumpets.

REVELATION 8:1–2 GNT

Silently I wait for you, O
God, in the quiet depths of
my open and expectant heart.
Amen.

GOD IS EVERYWHERE

I look behind me and you're there, then up ahead and you're there, too—your reassuring presence, coming and going.

PSALM 139:5 THE MESSAGE

Everywhere you are, God is. God is there in all the directions you take, no matter which way you choose to go. God is there in all the conditions of life, whatever their nature or intensity. God, who loves you enough to make you as special as you are, does not leave you alone at any time. God is at your side day to day and step by step.

You can think God isn't around, but that doesn't mean he isn't. You can mark God absent, if that's what you conclude, but you will be making the wrong notation in the roll book.

You might feel that God has abandoned you, but he hasn't done anything of the kind. God would never do that to you.

You have upheld me in my
integrity and set me in Your
presence forever.

PSALM 41:12 AMP

Dear God, thank you for sur-
rounding me all the time
with who you are.

Amen.

LISTEN TO YOUR HEART

Our soul waits for the LORD; He is our help and our shield. For our heart shall rejoice in Him, because we have trusted in His holy name.

PSALM 33:20–21 NKJV

God's favorite dwelling place is in your heart. He lives and speaks to you there. He tells you how special you are to him. In your heart, you know the truth about how much you mean to God.

In your heart, you have a powerful interaction with God. From there you can talk with God confidently about his will for you. From there you can speak clearly about your needs and can focus directly on the one who supplies your needs. Your heart is the holy place where you and God meet.

Your heart is where you can bask in God's presence and hear his words of love and wisdom. Listen to your heart.

You have put gladness in my heart, more than when their grain and new wine abound.

PSALM 4:7 NASB

Dear God, I am glad that you dwell in my heart.

Amen.

CLOSE THE DOOR

When you pray, you should go into your room and
close the door and pray to your Father who cannot be
seen. Your Father can see what is done in secret, and
he will reward you. MATTHEW 6:6 NCV

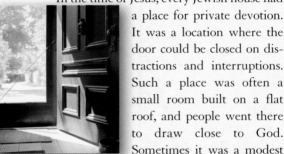

In the time of Jesus, every Jewish house had a place for private devotion. It was a location where the door could be closed on distractions and interruptions. Such a place was often a small room built on a flat roof, and people went there to draw close to God. Sometimes it was a modest space raised a story above the rest of the house where people retired to nourish their souls in the reality and certainty of God.

You have such a place. It is wherever you can go to be with God in a way you are unable to do anywhere else.

As you go to that place, you are excited about what will happen. You know your time there with God will be rich and fruitful.

Call to me and I will answer
you. I'll tell you marvelous
and wondrous things that
you could never figure out
on your own.

JEREMIAH 33:3 THE MESSAGE

Dear God, help me shut out
anything that would take your
place in my mind and heart.

Amen.

ALWAYS AVAILABLE

This is the confidence we have in approaching God: that if we ask anything according to his will, he hears us.

1 JOHN 5:14 NIV

You will never get a busy signal on God's prayer line. The circuits of heaven are never jammed.  You can have an audience with God at a stated time in a holy place, or you can talk to him as you run to the next thing in your life. You can get through to God anytime you want.

Ready and constant access to God is your birthright. By being always available, God shows how much you mean to him. You can count on God's focused attention because you count so much to God. God honors who you are to him by listening to everything you have to say.

You can talk to God because you know he listens to you. His ears are always outstretched in your direction.

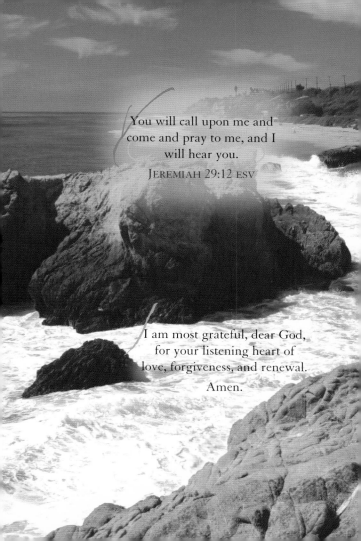

You will call upon me and come and pray to me, and I will hear you.

JEREMIAH 29:12 ESV

I am most grateful, dear God, for your listening heart of love, forgiveness, and renewal.

Amen.

SPEAK WITH YOUR FRIEND

The LORD spoke to Moses face to face as a man speaks with his friend.

EXODUS 33:11 NCV

Prayer is relational. It is talking to someone you know. There are no strangers in the prayer

room. When speaking to God in prayer, you can have the same kind of experience with God that Moses had— face to face. You can be friend with friend.

With God as your friend in prayer, you are never too hurt to look back, and you are never too scared to look ahead. With God as your friend in prayer, you can look within yourself and celebrate who you are and who you are becoming. You can feel close enough to God to open yourself up and let him come in.

When you go to God in prayer, you are in the presence of one you know and one who knows you.

Servants don't know what their master is doing, and so I don't speak to you as my servants. I speak to you as my friends, and I have told you everything that my Father has told me.

JOHN 15:15 CEV

Thank you, dear God, for being a friend closer and dearer than any other. You are my very best friend.

Amen.

OKAY NOW

You will show me the path that leads to life; your presence fills me with joy and brings me pleasure forever.

PSALM 16:11 GNT

Circumstances can be dire and forecasts bleak, but when you are close to God, you can be secure enough to step forward in your life with purpose and courage. You can have confidence to move toward goals and objectives, and know that God is with you.

As God accompanies you, he gives wisdom to your mind, resolve to your will, and joy to your heart. He reinforces that you belong to him. He makes known the many and varied resources he makes available to you. God's presence guarantees that you will never be alone and that you will never have to face anything by yourself.

You can stand tall because God lifts you up. You can stride confidently because God walks with you.

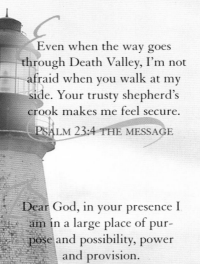

Even when the way goes through Death Valley, I'm not afraid when you walk at my side. Your trusty shepherd's crook makes me feel secure.

PSALM 23:4 THE MESSAGE

Dear God, in your presence I am in a large place of purpose and possibility, power and provision.

Amen.

PEACE AT THE CENTER

The peace that Christ gives is to guide you in the decisions you make; for it is to this peace that God has called you together in the one body.

COLOSSIANS 3:15 GNT

Peace in your heart makes your life beautiful and wonderful. It is the peace God gives when you draw close to him to receive his love and blessing. This peace counters the turbulence you have elsewhere in your life. It brings the stability of knowing you belong to God and the security of knowing he is with you always.

God's peace comes when you know how much God loves you, how far he goes to forgive you, how many ways he sustains you, and how many generous life opportunities he offers you. God's peace will guide you in the way you should go.

God puts the calm of his presence and the peace of his love at the center of your life.

You will experience God's peace, which is far more wonderful than the human mind can understand. His peace will guard your hearts and minds as you live in Christ Jesus.

PHILIPPIANS 4:7 NLT

Dear God, when I know you in my heart, I have peace in my life.

Amen.

NOT A WORD

Everyone kept quiet and listened as Barnabas and Paul told how God had given them the power to work a lot of miracles and wonders for the Gentiles.

ACTS 15:12 CEV

Silence invites God into your heart and ignites you with a passion for his closeness. It takes down the bars that the world's busyness and noise put on your soul and opens the door where God stands waiting to enter. Silence is a direct path to God's presence. Many of the wonderful gifts that come from God are given in silence.

When Elijah left a cave and went to a mountain to hear from God, he listened intently for the divine voice in blustery wind, trembling earthquake, and blistering fire. He heard from God, but not in any of that. God chose to speak to Elijah in absolute silence.

Silence is a condition in which God makes himself known to you.

The LORD was not in the
wind; and after the wind an
earthquake, but the LORD
was not in the earthquake;
and after the earthquake a
fire, but the LORD was not in
the fire; and after the fire a
sound of sheer silence.

1 KINGS 19:11–12 NRSV

Dear God, fade my words into
silence. Give me the gift of quiet.
Then I will hear you better.

Amen.

YOU CAN COUNT ON IT

My Presence will go with you,
and I will give you rest.

EXODUS 33:14 NIV

You can count on God's presence in your quiet moments. Time after time in Holy Scripture, God promises he will be present when you intentionally draw aside to meet him. God's presence is everywhere in the stories of the Bible. God makes the promise of his presence, and he keeps that promise. You can stand on the promise of God's presence to be with you.

God will make himself known to you as a living and bright reality. He will be at your side and will abide there in love and grace. He will move into your heart to embrace your life and guide your way. God is present to your needs.

God promises to take up daily residence in your heart.

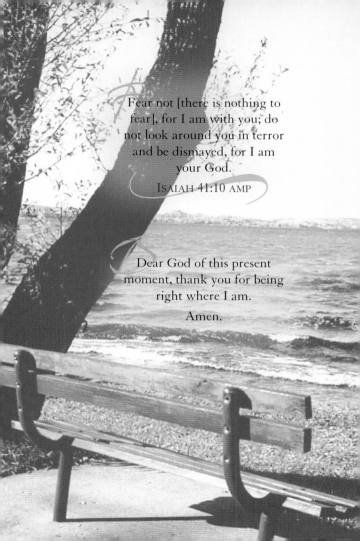

Fear not [there is nothing to fear], for I am with you; do not look around you in terror and be dismayed, for I am your God.

ISAIAH 41:10 AMP

Dear God of this present moment, thank you for being right where I am.

Amen.

MORE THAN HIS SHARE

Come to Me, all you who labor and are heavy-laden and overburdened, and I will cause you to rest. [I will ease and relieve and refresh your souls.]
MATTHEW 11:28 AMP

Whatever burden you have to carry, God will shoulder the better part of it. God will take the greater portion of your struggle on himself. He will bear the extra weight and move with you to resolution.

Imagine holding a glass of water and wondering how much it weighs. You don't know, but the longer you hold it, the more it seems to weigh. Hold it for a minute, and it's okay. But hold it for ten minutes, and your arm begins to ache. Hold it for an hour, and you might have to call an ambulance. But if you take the glass of water to a table and set it down, everything is okay again.

God will take your load on his back and give you rest.

Return, O my soul, to your
rest, for the LORD has dealt
bountifully with you.

PSALM 116:7 NRSV

Dear God, you lift my burdens with your love. Thank
you for helping me so much.
Amen.

Desire God

LORD, You have heard
the desire of the humble;
You will prepare their
heart; You will cause
Your ear to hear.

PSALM 10:17 NKJV

BUILDING BACK

Whoever there is among you of all His people, may his God be with him! Let him go up to Jerusalem which is in Judah and rebuild the house of the LORD.
EZRA 1:3 NASB

When you have disappointments and setbacks in your life, remember that such experiences provide a good foundation on which to regroup and rebuild. God honors that foundation with his spirit of renewal and his gift of strength.

When you call on and receive God's support and accept his help, a failure may turn out to be one of the best things that ever happens to you. It provides an opportunity to know who God is and what he can do. It introduces you to abilities, capacities, and aptitudes you didn't know you had. It lets you know how powerful your partnership with God is.

Failure put in the hands of God is the first step to something better. It is the ingredient that gives flavor to future success.

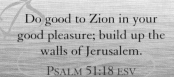

Do good to Zion in your good pleasure; build up the walls of Jerusalem.

PSALM 51:18 ESV

Dear God, grant me the courage to follow as you lead me from failure to success. Amen.

FIND A PLACE

You lead me to streams of peaceful water,
and you refresh my life.

PSALM 23:2–3 CEV

When you find a place where you can be alone with God, God will pour out his blessings  upon you. Locate a place where interruptions can be discouraged, distractions avoided, and potential disruptions prevented. Find a space where you and God can be together, just the two of you. Put a DO NOT DISTURB sign on the door of that place. Choose a setting that encourages meditation, prayer, and reflection.

You can hear God speak to you in such a quiet, private place. There you can experience the holy presence of God.

Early in his life, Jesus formed the habit of frequently going away into the hills for quiet prayer to his Father. He went somewhere still and private. He had a place.

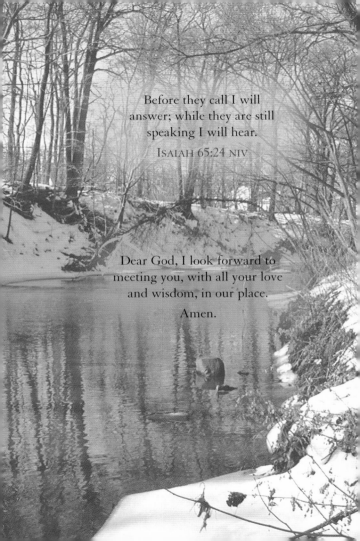

Before they call I will answer; while they are still speaking I will hear.

ISAIAH 65:24 NIV

Dear God, I look forward to meeting you, with all your love and wisdom, in our place.

Amen.

OPEN THE BOOK

Your word is a lamp to my feet and a light to my path. I have sworn and confirmed that I will keep Your righteous judgments.

PSALM 119:105–106 NKJV

You have a readily available manual for the time you spend close to God. In that manual are instructions about prayer, meditation, and reflection. In that same manual you will learn what it means to have a heart for God. On its pages are clear directions for a life lived with God.

You will read about the spiritual journeys of very real people, just like you, and you can discern from their stories how to feel the closeness of God. In this manual, you will find directions and signposts for your walk with God. This manual is the Bible, the greatest how-to book ever written.

Read of God's love, affection, and desire for you in the Bible.

God's words are pure words,
pure silver words refined
seven times in the fires of his
word-kiln.

PSALM 12:6 THE MESSAGE

Dear God, I open your book
and find in it your word, your
way, and your will for me.
Amen.

SOMETHING ON THE WAY

Peter said, "I don't have any silver or gold! But I will give you what I do have. In the name of Jesus Christ from Nazareth, get up and start walking."

ACTS 3:6 CEV

As you draw close to God, you sense something new in the air. You feel the breath of God's Spirit coming toward where you are.

In a painting of the blind man at Jericho by the French master Nicolas Poussin, you can sense the expectancy of the one kneeling before Jesus for healing. His left hand is outstretched, palms open toward Jesus. His right hand is raised and extended in anticipation. The right leg of the blind man is posed to take the first step into a new day of light and wholeness. He has come to Jesus, fully expecting to see.

Dawn arrives and you are standing on the edge of new possibilities. You have absolute assurance that something special is on the way.

On the following day they
came to Caesarea. Cornelius
was waiting for them and
had called together his
relatives and close friends.

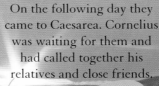

ACTS 10:24 NCV

When I realize who you are
and what you can do, dear
God, my expectations are
always high.

Amen.

GIVE GOD GLORY

Hallelujah! It's a good thing to sing praise to our God; praise is beautiful, praise is fitting.

PSALM 147:1 THE MESSAGE

A secretary who had been especially busy bowed her head at her desk and said, "God, I

think the stapler is your greatest invention." A good use of your time with God is to praise him for everything. Praise God, who gives you all you have.

A minister had just started his Sunday sermon when it started to thunder and lightning. Rain poured down in wild torrents. "God is wonderful!" he told the congregation. "While all of us are sitting here dry and comfortable, he's out there in the parking lot washing our cars for us!"

Find phrases for your praises. Create many and varied ways to say thank-you to God. You can't say enough praises to God.

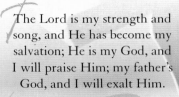

The Lord is my strength and song, and He has become my salvation; He is my God, and I will praise Him; my father's God, and I will exalt Him.

EXODUS 15:2 NKJV

Dear God, I raise my praise to you for all you do for me and all you are to me.

Amen.

HEAVEN IN YOUR HEART

Our hearts brim with joy since we've taken for our own his holy name.

PSALM 33:21 THE MESSAGE

You can have a little piece of heaven right now. Go somewhere to be alone with God. Talk with and listen to him, and he will put his joy in your heart. When you are with God, you will experience the spark of his love and the promise of heaven in your life. That spark will warm your spirit when you feel cold and weary, and it will provide a light to your path when you are confused and misdirected.

The joy of God's presence knows no boundaries. You can experience it anytime and anywhere and enjoy God's love and grace.

You can taste a bit of heaven when you intentionally put yourself before God. God will visit you in that moment and suffuse your heart with his love.

I, through the abundance of
your steadfast love, will enter
your house, I will bow down
toward your holy temple in
awe of you.

PSALM 5:7 NRSV

Dear God, when I know
your presence in my heart
and life, all the way to
heaven is heaven.

Amen.

A SPONGE IN THE OCEAN

God is actually not far from any one of us; as some-
one has said, "In him we live and move and exist."

ACTS 17:27–28 GNT

Attempting to communicate the extent and scope of God to people standing on an Athens hill, Paul gathered up the sentiment of ancient poets and spoke of living and moving and existing in God. All of life, he said, is within God. There is no other context.

When you were a child, you may have thought God existed in space. It is truer, however, that space is in God. Everything is in God. God holds all creation in his palm. God holds the whole world and every-thing in it. That includes you. As a sponge is in the ocean, you are in God. Your truest and most authentic dwelling place is in God.

It is inside the love and providence of God that you live, move, and exist.

The LORD looks at the world
from his throne in heaven,
and he watches us all.

PSALM 33:13–14 CEV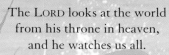

Dear God, thank you for
including everyone in the
reach of your embracing love.
Amen.

YOU ARE SPECIAL

He brought me forth also into a large place; He was delivering me because He was pleased with me and delighted in me.

PSALM 18:19 AMP

Take a minute to consider how much God thinks of you. Other people may put you down on occasion, but that'll never happen with God. The people whom you work with, and perhaps even those you live with, may not always understand what you are trying to say or do, but God knows and understands.

You may give yourself a hard time on occasion, but you can count on God to affirm and applaud you. When God made you, he took particular care to create you as a unique individual and an outstanding person. Nothing God creates is ordinary. You are extraordinary. You make the world special simply by being in it.

God gave a lot of thought to you. God knows that you are worth it.

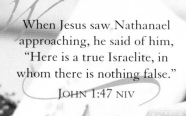

When Jesus saw Nathanael
approaching, he said of him,
"Here is a true Israelite, in
whom there is nothing false."

JOHN 1:47 NIV

Dear God, thank you for
valuing me the way you do.
Thank you for making me
feel important.

Amen.

MASKS OFF

The Lord told him, "Samuel, don't think Eliab is the one just because he's tall and handsome. . . . People judge others by what they look like, but I judge people by what is in their hearts."

1 SAMUEL 16:7 CEV

At the Mardi Gras Museum in New Orleans, a large glass case holds various masks used in past carnival celebrations over a time span of many years. A printed legend propped inside the case called *The Power of the Mask* offers this explanation: "A new face and different attire allows a masker to transcend everyday life and construct a new self, an altered psyche."

God, however, invites you to do just the opposite. He invites you to take off your masks, both the public and private ones. He wants to see you as you are. He wants you to see yourself as you are.

There need be no hiding in the presence of God, for you can be real with him all the time.

He didn't need any help in
seeing right through them.

JOHN 2:25 THE MESSAGE

Dear God, I know that when I
try to hide I am lost, but when
I come to you, I am found.

Amen.

WHERE THE POWER IS

Be exalted, O LORD, in Your strength; we will sing and praise Your power.

PSALM 21:13 NASB

After a destructive hurricane hit their city and there was no electrical power, people scur-ried to purchase generators that ran on diesel fuel. The various capacities of those generators were able to keep refrigerators and freezers going, provide lighting and air conditioning for houses, get businesses going, and perform other needed functions. The generators used an inordinate amount of fuel, however, and the fuel kept running out. After several days, electric-power companies moved through the city connecting houses to a power source that was steady and constant.

The constant and steady power you need for your life comes from God. You do not find it in substitutes. You find it in the bedrock grace of almighty God. God is the source of your power for living.

They will see the Son of Man coming in clouds with great (kingly) power and glory (majesty and splendor).

MARK 13:26 AMP

God of power and might, thank you for giving me the clout and strength I need for life every day.

Amen.

GOD'S PERFECT ATTENDANCE

*You wisely and tenderly lead me, and
then you bless me.*
PSALM 73:24 THE MESSAGE

God is always with you. You can count on
it. He is beside you in the reality of your life. You

are always in his care. God
takes no vacations from his
care of you. He takes no hol-
idays; he takes no leaves of
absence.

Old Faithful is one of
the country's most popular
tourist attractions. Oddly
enough, it isn't the largest or
most spectacular geyser in
Yellowstone. What makes it so popular with so
many is that it is uniquely regular in its erup-
tions. It is dependable. People can count on it to
act like a geyser is supposed to act.

The faithfulness of God is particularized in
your life by his steady and constant attention to
who you are and what you do.

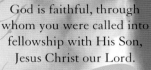

God is faithful, through whom you were called into fellowship with His Son, Jesus Christ our Lord.

1 CORINTHIANS 1:9 NASB

Dear God, thank you for your unquestionable faithfulness. Thank you for never taking your eyes off me.

Amen.

CLAIM GOD'S PRESENCE

[The Lord] said, "My presence will go with you, and I will give you rest." And [Moses] said to him, "If your presence will not go, do not carry us up from here."

EXODUS 33:14–15 NRSV

In speaking to God plainly and boldly, Moses set a precedent for how you can talk to God. Moses made it okay for you to let God know exactly where you stand on the issue of his presence. Moses knew he had a right to claim the presence of God, and so do you. It is a claim God expects you to make.

When God wanted the children of Israel to go forward toward a holy land, Moses made sure that God's name was on the traveling list before he started out. Moses forthrightly told God that he wanted to be assured of his presence and that Moses could count him in.

Ask God to be with you wherever you go. He is waiting for your request.

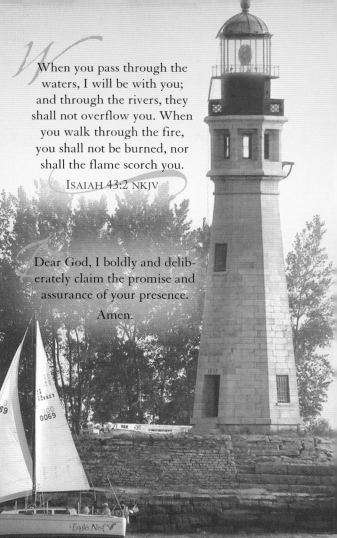

When you pass through the waters, I will be with you; and through the rivers, they shall not overflow you. When you walk through the fire, you shall not be burned, nor shall the flame scorch you.

ISAIAH 43:2 NKJV

Dear God, I boldly and deliberately claim the promise and assurance of your presence.

Amen.

SOME REMINDERS

You must make this Tabernacle and its furnishings exactly according to the plans I will show you.

EXODUS 25:9 NLT

When God wanted his people to know he was with them, he chose to occupy a tent as the meeting place. In fact, it was called the tent of meeting. It was the place where God and his people got together. Inside the tent was an ark of specific dimensions and decoration that represented God's glory. The imagery reminded the people that God was with them.

You need reminders of the presence of God in the place where you meet God. Have an open Bible as a reminder that God speaks to you. Light a votive candle to symbolize your continuing prayer. Place a cross prominently to indicate how much God loves you.

A symbol is a reminder of something much greater than itself. It points you to God.

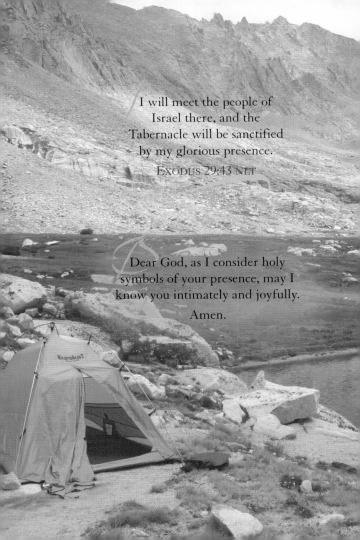

I will meet the people of
Israel there, and the
Tabernacle will be sanctified
by my glorious presence.

Exodus 29:43 NLT

Dear God, as I consider holy
symbols of your presence, may I
know you intimately and joyfully.

Amen.

SEE THE LIGHT

Jesus once again addressed them: "I am the world's Light. No one who follows me stumbles around in the darkness. I provide plenty of light to live in."

JOHN 8:12 THE MESSAGE

The first thing Harlan does in his prayer place is to light a candle. He begins each time of meditation this way. Harlan wants to symbolize that he experiences the presence of God as light. He begins his meeting with God focused on the illumination God provides. He believes God's light is strong enough to eliminate any darkness he might be experiencing.

Light is God's nature. That is why in the Jewish tabernacle a perpetual lamp burned, a light that never went out. It was there to remind people of the ever-present light of God.

Nothing eliminates the darkness of the world like the light of God.

The people who walked in darkness have seen a great light. For those who lived in a land of deep shadows— light! sunbursts of light!

ISAIAH 9:2 THE MESSAGE

Dear God, your love for me lights up my life. I praise your holy name.

Amen.

Seek God

This is what the LORD says
to the nation of Israel:
"Come to me and live."

AMOS 5:4 NCV

RIGHT WORD, RIGHT TIME

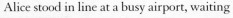

The LORD says, "I will make you wise and show you where to go. I will guide you and watch over you."
PSALM 32:8 NCV

Alice stood in line at a busy airport, waiting to check in with the reservation clerk. She was relocating across the country to begin a new job. It was a job she had long wanted, but Alice had many doubts about her ability to fulfill the job's varied responsibilities. *Is the job too much for me?* she wondered. *Have I made a big mistake?*

Alice was second in line to check in when the elderly man in front of her got his ticket and turned back. He put a firm hand on Alice's shoulder as he passed by and warmly said to her, "God bless you. I'm sure everything is going to be all right."

God sends people with words of encouragement at the time you need them.

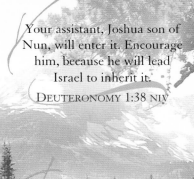

Your assistant, Joshua son of
Nun, will enter it. Encourage
him, because he will lead
Israel to inherit it.

DEUTERONOMY 1:38 NIV

Thank you, dear God, for
the people you send to me
with your word for my life.

Amen.

> *Remember that the person who plants few seeds will have a small crop; the one who plants many seeds will have a large crop.*
>
> 2 CORINTHIANS 9:6 GNT

When you give to God's people, God gives himself to you. The more the early church gave to those in need, the greater the blessings it received. When they gave to others, God gave to them.

Many years ago, a limousine pulled up to where a beggar sat. A well-dressed and obviously rich man in the limousine asked the beggar to share his rice with him. The beggar was taken aback by the request and very grudgingly gave the man three pieces of rice. That night, the beggar discovered three sparkling pieces of gold in his bowl. Shaking his head, he lamented, "If I had only given more."

You release the flow of God's blessings to you by letting the blessings you have go through you.

Bring the full tithes into the storehouse, that there may be food in my house. And thereby put me to the test, says the LORD of hosts, if I will not open the windows of heaven for you and pour down for you a blessing until there is no more need.

MALACHI 3:10 ESV

Dear God, I receive every time I give. Your blessings know the way to me.

Amen.

ASK GOD FOR HELP

Rescue me from my enemies, O LORD, for I hide myself in you. Teach me to do your will, for you are my God.
                                    PSALM 143:9–10 NIV

Asking is God's plan to get you to go to him for help. The Bible clearly emphasizes the importance of asking in order to receive. The repetition of this in word and story leaves no doubt as to how God wants you to act when you have a need. God wants you to ask. Charles Spurgeon said, "Whether we like it or not, asking is the rule of the kingdom."

There is always something to be gained when you ask God for help. Cry out your need to God. He will honor your request. He will strengthen you for your tasks, give insight for your relationships, enlighten your mind, and fill your heart.

In the Lord's Prayer, you are encouraged six times to ask God for help.

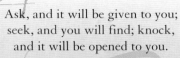

Ask, and it will be given to you;
seek, and you will find; knock,
and it will be opened to you.

MATTHEW 7:7 NASB

Dear God, I am grateful that
you are ready to give when I
am ready to ask.

Amen.

REMEMBER OTHERS

I will certainly not sin against the LORD by ending my prayers for you.

1 SAMUEL 12:23 NLT

Talk to God about other people. Talk to him about who is physically sick and the form of

that sickness. Tell God who is under emotional stress and the cause of their anxiety. Tell God about the people you know who are financially strung out, unable to take care of their families as they want to. Tell God who is experiencing a shattered dream and can't seem to get up off the floor.

Talking to God and telling him about others is to intercede on their behalf. "Intercession," said Andrew Murray in his book *A Ministry of Intercession,* "is the most perfect form of prayer."

Lift the names and conditions of others to God. Let God know what they need.

He is able also to save forever those who draw near to God through Him, since He always lives to make intercession for them.

HEBREWS 7:25 NASB

Dear God, I bring the needs of others to you in faith, confidence, and obedience.

Amen.

BELIEVE BIG

Jesus said to him, "Thomas, because you have seen Me, you have believed. Blessed are those who have not seen and yet have believed."

JOHN 20:29 NKJV

Believing big things about God is the beginning of a new and exciting life in God. When you believe big about God, a new and fresh spirit comes to you. Such a belief invigorates your daily walk. Your decisions are clearer. Your staying power more adequately matches your starting power.

When you believe big about God, you act on the premise of a capable and competent God. You hope more; you dream more. You dare more; you do more. To believe something is to act as if it is so. One person with a strong belief has a power equal to many people who have only interests.

Your belief about what God can do puts you in touch with the power of God to get it done.

Immediately the father of the
child cried out, "I believe;
help my unbelief!"

MARK 9:24 NRSV

Dear God, I believe you are
able to do important work in
me and significant work
through me.

Amen.

BEGIN AND END

*The LORD is your protector, there at your right side
to shade you from the sun. You won't be harmed by
the sun during the day or by the moon at night.*

PSALM 121:5–6 CEV

Psalm 121, sung by people going to Jerusalem for major festivals, speaks frequently of God's ability to "keep" you. There are six direct references to that idea. God is able to keep you, the psalmist said, because he is always on the job for you.

God is present as you begin and end each day. He is there when the sun comes up, and he is there when it has gone down. As your day begins, God is there to guide and direct you. As it ends, he is there to watch over and protect you. God wakes you in the morning and puts you to bed at night.

God begins and ends each day with you. He invites you to begin and end each day with him.

Blessed be the Lord, who
daily bears our burden.

PSALM 68:19 NASB

Dear God, thank you for being
present to me with your love
and encouragement all day long.

Amen.

GOD GUIDES YOU

He scatters His bright clouds. And they swirl about, being turned by His guidance, that they may do whatever He commands them.

JOB 37:11–12 NKJV

Guidance is high on the list of what God likes to do for you. He likes to get you on the  road, acquaint you with its twists and turns, warn you of soft shoulders and slippery surfaces, and put map and itinerary on your lap so you can reach your destination and fulfill your destiny. God gives you directions to follow. God points the way for you that he knows so well.

The Bible is filled with stories of divine guidance. Abraham was guided to a new land, Moses was guided back to it, Jesus was directed into the wilderness, and Paul was led to Macedonia to take the gospel to Europe. Nothing has changed.

Your story is one of God's instruction and direction. God leads you each day.

You're my cave to hide in,
my cliff to climb. Be my safe
leader, be my true mountain
guide.

PSALM 31:3 THE MESSAGE

Thank you, dear God, for
knowing the way I should go
and for showing it to me one
step at a time.

Amen.

IN THE MORNING

I tell you the truth, whoever believes has eternal life.

JOHN 6:47 NCV

Getting close to God and staying there gives you a sense of eternal destiny. Your time of  prayer and moments of reflection have about them an eternal dimension. God speaks to you of forever. He assures you of a life that never ends.

A man who was known for his deep faith found out he had a serious disease and would not live long. He sat down and wrote a letter to his best friend. He told his friend, "I learned today of my impending death. Before you read this, I may already be in heaven. Don't bother to write; I'll see you in the morning."

You are assured of a home in heaven, where you will live with God forever.

I write this to you who believe
in (adhere to, trust in, and rely
on) the name of the Son of God
[in the peculiar services and
blessings conferred by Him on
men], so that you may know
[with settled and absolute
knowledge] that you [already]
have life, yes, eternal life.

1 JOHN 5:13 AMP

Dear God, thank you for giving
me a life that will never end.

Amen.

IT TAKES BOTH

Trust in the LORD and do good; dwell in the land and enjoy safe pasture. Delight yourself in the LORD and he will give you the desires of your heart. Commit your way to the LORD; trust in him and he will do this.

PSALM 37:3–5 NIV

When a fine artist takes the hand of a promising student and guides it on the canvas,  the brushstroke is more the teacher's than the student's. The student holds the brush and makes a motion of the hand, but the teacher's touch comes through to the painting. Much honor and praise belong to the teacher.

But there is honor and praise for the student as well. The student has put himself in the teacher's capable hands, has made himself malleable to the teacher's touch. The student has yielded to the motion and direction of the teacher. The surrender of the student to the teacher brings wonderful and beautiful results.

Your attitudes and actions are always better when you let God guide them with his hand and heart.

Teach me to follow you, and
I will obey your truth.
Always keep me faithful.

PSALM 86:11 CEV

Dear God, I feel the inspiring
and directing touch of your
hand on mine.

Amen.

HOPE BURNS ON

You are my hope; O Lord GOD, You are my
confidence from my youth.

PSALM 71:5 NASB

An ancient Ethiopian legend tells about a shepherd boy name Alemayu. One time he  was stranded on a frozen mountain, clothed only in a thin cloak. After a long and treacherous night, he returned home. The villagers were amazed that he had survived as well as he had. When asked to explain, he said, "The night was bitter cold. The sky was pitch-dark. Then, far off, I saw a shepherd's fire on another mountain. I kept my eyes on the red glow in the distance and hoped of being warm."

Hope is a fire that burns in your heart and won't go out even in dark and difficult times. Hope tells you tomorrow will be better.

Always have a supply of hope on hand to help you plan your tomorrows.

What a God we have! And how fortunate we are to have him, this Father of our Master Jesus! Because Jesus was raised from the dead, we've been given a brand-new life and have everything to live for.

1 Peter 1:3 The Message

Dear God, I know that my hope is a forecast of your presence and a foretaste of your power.

Amen.

YOU ARE A PEARL

God has not given us a spirit of fear, but of power and of love and of a sound mind.

2 TIMOTHY 1:7 NKJV

An oyster embeds itself in the mire of the ocean floor. A pearl grows slowly and gradually within the mucous of the inside of the oyster's shell. This hardly seems an appropriate setting for something as beautiful as a pearl. Think of the lovely pearls you have seen; they shine and sparkle despite their early environment.

No matter what kind of bad situation your life may be in, God sees beyond that. He sees you as the valuable and worthy person you really are. God goes beyond your assessment and that of others to his own appraisal of your merit and significance. God sees the pearl.

God looks beyond where you and others watch. He always sees something special in you.

The kingdom of heaven is like a merchant in search of fine pearls, who, on finding one pearl of great value, went and sold all that he had and bought it.

MATTHEW 13:45–46 ESV

Dear God, I am grateful that you look far enough in me to see what is there.

Amen.

YOU ARE LOVED

I give you a new commandment, that you love one another. Just as I have loved you, you also should love one another.

JOHN 13:34 NRSV

One afternoon, several teenagers were playing basketball in a backyard. A dispute broke out, and the youth whose backyard it was grabbed the ball and roughly ordered the others to leave.

Then he saw his mother looking out the back window. She had heard and seen everything. He slumped in to where his mother stood at the sink. "Mom, I'm sorry I acted like that," he said. She took his hands and said, "I didn't like what you did at all, and you certainly know better than to act that way." Then she hugged him and said, "I love you." He knew his mother loved him. There was no doubt about that.

There is nothing like someone loving you no matter what you have done.

I will heal their waywardness and
love them freely, for my anger
has turned away from them.

HOSEA 14:4 NIV

Dear God, thank you for
those you send who love me
no matter what I do.

Amen.

WELL MADE

You are the one who put me together inside my mother's body, and I praise you because of the wonderful way you created me.

PSALM 139:13–14 CEV

Look at your body and think about how wonderfully God has made you. Stretch your arms, flex your fingers, and consider what they enable you to do. Turn your hand over, and remember that no one else in the world has the same fingerprints as you. No one else has your voice print or your genetic code. Listen to your heart beat. Think of its exactness and precision, its regularity and reliability. Consider all the capabilities of the body God made for you.

Thank God for how well he made your body. Thank him for what you are able to do and where you are able to go because of your body.

You are a well-made work of God. When God made your body, he knew what he was doing.

*W*orthy are You, our Lord and God, to receive the glory and the honor and dominion, for You created all things; by Your will they were [brought into being] and were created.

REVELATION 4:11 AMP

Dear God, thank you for the gift of my body. May I use it to make your love known in the world.

Amen.

PRAYER GETS IT DONE

From now on, whatever you request along the lines of who I am and what I am doing, I'll do it. That's how the Father will be seen for who he is in the Son. I mean it.

JOHN 14:13 THE MESSAGE

Prayer is practical. It gets things done. People would ask Charles Spurgeon to explain his phenomenal power as a preacher, and he would reply in an economy of words, "My people pray for me." To light a fire of effectiveness in your life, kneel in prayer. Dwight L. Moody said, "Every great movement of the kingdom can be traced to one kneeling figure."

Prayer is an uplook that profoundly changes the outlook. It is a fountain from which you drink wisdom for the day and find strength for the way. Its water nourishes your mind to purpose and your will to power.

Through prayer, you put yourself in God's hands to be held in love and sent forth in power.

Do not worry about anything,
but in everything by prayer
and supplication with thanksgiving let your requests be
made known to God.

PHILIPPIANS 4:6 NRSV

Dear God, through the gift
of your power in my life, I
can get it done.

Amen.

Love God

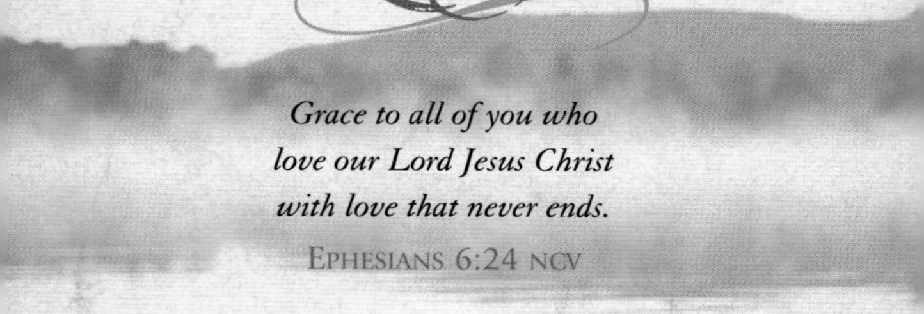

*Grace to all of you who
love our Lord Jesus Christ
with love that never ends.*

Ephesians 6:24 ncv

 OUT OF THE SEA

Bow down Your ear to me, deliver me speedily! Be my Rock of refuge, a strong Fortress to save me!

PSALM 31:2 AMP

In the first years of the space program, military personnel in helicopters would rescue astronauts whose space capsule had splashed down into the large and encompassing sea. They would track the capsule's location, fly there, and use a pulley system to lift the astronauts securely into the helicopter. Then the helicopter would fly the astronauts to safety.

God knows when you have splashed down in a threatening sea. He sees the difficulties you get into sometimes. He is aware of the problems that come your way. There is nothing about your challenges, trials, and tests that escapes the attention of God. God knows when you need to be picked up and rescued.

God knows when you need his help. He lifts you up and makes you safe.

The Lord will rescue me
from every evil deed and
bring me safely into his
heavenly kingdom.

2 TIMOTHY 4:18 ESV

Dear God, thank you for
every time you have pulled
me out of a bad place.

Amen.

SAY AMEN

No matter how many promises God has made, they are "Yes" in Christ. And so through him the "Amen" is spoken by us to the glory of God.

2 CORINTHIANS 1:20 NIV

Have you been in a church service when someone in the congregation says amen when the pastor says something? The pastor makes another point, the person again says amen. The person agrees with what the pastor has said, and he gives voice to his agreement. Sometimes a pastor will encourage the congregation to participate: "Say amen."

Say amen to God's claim on your life and his call in your life. Agree with who God says you are. Be in accord with what God wants you to do. Be enthusiastic in your agreement. Say amen to God's purpose and plan for you.

Say amen to who you are, and to the gifts of God's grace you have.

Grow in the grace and knowledge of our Lord and Savior Jesus Christ. To him be the glory both now and to the day of eternity. Amen.

2 PETER 3:18 ESV

Dear God, I agree with both your short-term and long-range plans for me.

Amen.

HEAD OVER HEELS IN LOVE

Jesus answered: Love the Lord your God with all your heart, soul, and mind. This is the first and most important commandment.

MATTHEW 22:37–38 CEV

You love God because of his infinite goodness in your life. You love God because he is your Father and you are his child. You love him because he created you and has a meaningful plan for your life. You love God because he first loved you.

Legend has it that a wealthy merchant heard a great deal about Paul. The merchant went to Rome to visit Paul in prison. Timothy arranged it, and the man spent several hours with Paul. Outside the cell, as he was leaving, the man asked Timothy, "What's the secret of this man's power?" Timothy smiled and said, "Paul is in love."

When you know how much you mean to God, you fall head over heels in love with God.

No eye has seen, nor ear heard,
nor the human heart conceived,
what God has prepared for
those who love him.

1 CORINTHIANS 2:9 NRSV

Dear God, you mean every-
thing in the world to me. I
love you more than I can say.

Amen.

LITTLE THINGS

God has made everything beautiful for its own time.
ECCLESIASTES 3:11 NLT

A woman asked a famous Bible teacher a question that had long been on her mind. She said, "Do you think we ought to pray about the little things in everyday life?" The renowned teacher responded immediately. "Can you think of anything in your life that is unimportant to God?" She couldn't think of a thing.

No problem you have is too small for your prayers to God. No difficulty you experience is too minor to talk to God about. He invites you to tell him about the small occurrences. God has an open ear for you and your life. When you talk to God, don't leave anything out.

God is interested in everything in your life. It is all vitally important to him. Nothing is too small.

Well done, good and faithful
servant; you were faithful
over a few things, I will make
you ruler over many things.

MATTHEW 25:21 NKJV

Dear God, I am comforted by your
concern for all the happenings
and issues of my life.

Amen.

GET IN TUNE

I have given you this as an example, so that you should do [in your turn] what I have done to you.

JOHN 13:15 AMP

A man who lived alone had a cello he played for his own enjoyment. He played his cello when he was happy to celebrate the good things in his life. He played it when he was distressed to express his sadness and gloom. Sometimes he played his cello for no obvious reason at all.

Every now and then, his cello got out of tune. When it did, he called a friend at a radio station and asked him to broadcast the true and precise tone of A. By that authentic tone, he tuned his cello and was ready to play again.

Jesus is the tone by which you can tune your life. Get your pitch from him every day.

My friends, I want you to follow
my example and learn from
others who closely follow the
example we set for you.

PHILIPPIANS 3:17 CEV

Dear God, thank you that
Jesus walks before me so I
can know which way to go.

Amen.

SOLITUDE STRENGTHENS

*After he had dismissed them, he went up on a
mountainside by himself to pray. When evening
came, he was there alone.*

MATTHEW 14:23 NIV

Solitude can increase your capacity for
experiencing the presence of
God. "Without solitude,"
Henri Nouwen said, "it is vir-
tually impossible to live a spiritual life." Solitude expresses
the beauty, meaning, and
glory of being alone with
God. Jesus understood this.
The world had waited thou-
sands of years for him to come, and one of the
first things he did was to announce that he
wanted forty days to be alone with God.

Solitude makes you aware of whether you
are living from the outside in or from the inside
out. When you listen to your heart in rich
moments of solitude, you are drawn to significant activity.

Solitude enriches your spiritual resources. It
is purposeful and productive.

When evening came, the boat
was out on the sea, and he
was alone on the land.

MARK 6:47 NRSV

Dear God, in my solitude I
am alone with you, your
grace, and your wisdom.

Amen.

SAY THANK-YOU

Bless the LORD, O my soul; and all that is within me, bless His holy name! Bless the LORD, O my soul, and forget not all His benefits.

PSALM 103:1–2 NKJV

When you were young and someone gave you something, your dad or mom would remind you, "Now, what do you say?" They wanted you to express gratitude for what you had received. Think of how generous God is to you and how grateful you are to him. Take out a pencil and paper and write down a list of your blessings. The psalmist tells you to not forget any of them.

Gratitude comes when you take time to count up your past and present gifts and benefits. It is a fundamental response to God's grace. Prayer reaches its highest level as gratitude.

Gratitude is the heart's memory of what God has done for you. The most complete prayer is a grateful thought toward heaven.

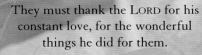

They must thank the LORD for his constant love, for the wonderful things he did for them.

PSALM 107:8 GNT

Dear God, when I think of what you do for me, my heart is lifted in gratitude and my voice in praise.

Amen.

A GREAT INVESTMENT

Be steadfast, immovable, always abounding in the
work of the Lord, knowing that your toil is not in
vain in the Lord.

1 CORINTHIANS 15:58 NASB

The greatest investment you can make is to
give who you are and what you have to God.

You will make no wiser
investment than to com-
mit your strengths and
resources to God. The
psychiatrist Paul Tournier
understood the return on
this investment when he
said it is commitment that "creates a person."

Not only does commitment enhance and
enrich who you are as a person, but it also nourishes and actualizes God's will in the world.
Your commitment gets God's work done. It lets
people know how much God loves them. It
inspires them to love God back and to serve him
in every way they can.

Commitment is an investment in your gifts
and in God's power.

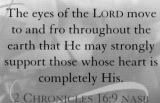

The eyes of the LORD move
to and fro throughout the
earth that He may strongly
support those whose heart is
completely His.

2 CHRONICLES 16:9 NASB

Dear God, keep me focused
on my responsibilities, obli-
gations, and commitments.

Amen.

REST UP

Come to me, all of you who are weary and carry heavy burdens, and I will give you rest.

MATTHEW 11:28 NLT

Look at a sheet of orchestral music and you will see a mark called a *rest*. It means you are to  quit playing for a brief count. You sit quiet and still with your instrument on your lap. This inactivity does not mean you have come to the end of the composition, however. There is more music to play, and you are getting ready to play it.

To live a good and influential life, you need rests and stops along the way. You need times when you are getting ready for what is to come. Jesus recognized those times as opportunities to put down your heavy burdens and find renewal in him.

A rest is that time and occasion when you get ready to make more music.

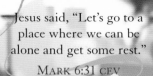

Jesus said, "Let's go to a place where we can be alone and get some rest."

MARK 6:31 CEV

Dear God, thank you for refreshing, renewing, and revitalizing times of rest.

Amen.

UP TO YOU

I heard the voice of the Lord, saying, Whom shall I send? And who will go for Us? Then said I, Here am I; send me.

ISAIAH 6:8 AMP

God causes wonderful and significant things to happen in your life. He blesses and gifts you in many ways. Then it is up to you to respond to what God has done. God's touch on your life wakes you to obligation, responsibility, and commitment. God moves in you, and then you move out and on for God.

When an alarm clock goes off in the morning, it wakes you up. But that's as much as an alarm clock can do. It cannot drag you out of bed. Getting up is your responsibility. God touches your heart with presence and call. It is then up to you to respond in faith and dedication.

God acts in your life, and waits for the response of your obedience and trust.

Commit to the LORD
whatever you do, and
your plans will succeed.

PROVERBS 16:3 NIV

Dear God, help me to take
whatever is given and make
it large for you.

Amen.

HAVEN AND HARBOR

If you are standing before the altar in the Temple, offering a sacrifice to God, and you suddenly remember that someone has something against you, leave your sacrifice there beside the altar. Go and be reconciled to that person.

MATTHEW 5:23–24 NLT

Your inside time with God has outside implications. Prayer is both a haven in which you rest and a harbor from which you sail. One time, Jesus and three of his disciples had a glorious spiritual experience on top of a mountain. Much to the disciples' dismay, Jesus made them get off the mountain to go down and help a sick boy in the valley.

God uses your close times with him to equip you for service in the world. Prayer sensitizes you and helps you recognize where you are needed. It opens doors in your mind and heart and will lead you to others.

Prayer enlarges your heart and makes it big enough to hold those who need you most.

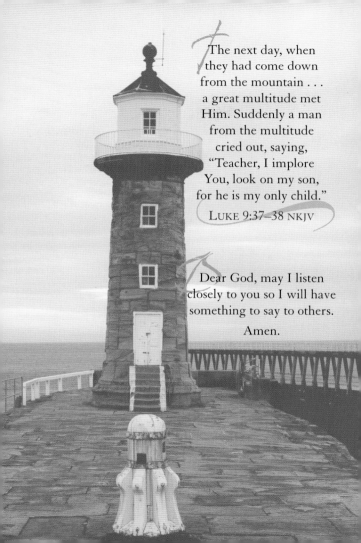

The next day, when they had come down from the mountain . . . a great multitude met Him. Suddenly a man from the multitude cried out, saying, "Teacher, I implore You, look on my son, for he is my only child."

LUKE 9:37–38 NKJV

Dear God, may I listen closely to you so I will have something to say to others.

Amen.

SECURITY SYSTEM

*The name of the Lord is a strong tower; the
[consistently] righteous man [upright and in
right standing with God] runs into it and is safe.*

The greatest security system in the world is
God. With him by your side,
you have confidence that
things will be okay. With God
beside you, you can handle
whatever pops up. God
accompanies you with the
power of his competence, and
you take comfort in this
knowledge. You can't go any-
where that God doesn't go along with you.

Security in God is like having an electric
fence built around your property to keep out
harmful intrusions. It is like an alarm system
that goes off when you need to be alerted to
danger and risk. It is like having someone with
a badge of authority go with you everywhere.

God's presence is a security system that
helps you smell the smoke and avoid the fire.

I have set the LORD always before me. Because he is at my right hand, I will not be shaken.

PSALM 16:8 NIV

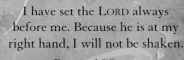

No matter what I go through, O God, you go through it with me. Where I am, you are.

Amen.

JUST AS YOU ARE

> *Behold, now is "the acceptable time," behold,*
> *now is "the day of salvation."*
>
> 2 CORINTHIANS 6:2 NASB

Charlotte Elliott, artist, singer, and composer, was a vivacious young woman. But when this talented and spirited woman was just thirty years old, a devastating illness made her an invalid. She became depressed and listless. She gave up every activity, turned away from all creativity.

One day Caesar Milan, a well-known evangelist, visited her. Understanding Charlotte's situation, he told her she must come to God right then just as she was. Charlotte Elliott responded to what Caesar Milan said and instantly placed her faith and illness in God's hands. She experienced tranquillity and bliss that day that lasted the rest of her life.

To express the joy of her coming to God, Charlotte Elliott wrote the great hymn "Just As I Am."

It is now time for you to wake
up from your sleep, because
our salvation is nearer now
than when we first believed.

ROMANS 13:11 NCV

Dear God, I come to you
right now, just as I am. You
accept, receive, and love me.

Amen.

A BIG GOD

Powerful is your arm! Strong is your hand! Your right hand is lifted high in glorious strength.

PSALM 89:13 NLT

Someone asked the movie director John Huston what was the toughest subject he ever had to work with in making a motion picture. He said it was the Bible stories, especially the creation scene and the flood scene in the movie *The Bible*. "I had a terrible time making them," he said. "I really don't know how God managed it." God managed it because he is almighty.

God's sovereignty over all of life means your life is divinely ordained and profoundly significant. God has written his will and way for you into your very being. Your response is of major importance and foremost consequence.

God made you special and important. He gave you what it takes.

The God who made the
world and everything in it is
the Lord of heaven and earth
and does not live in temples
built by hands.

ACTS 17:24 NIV

I fall at your feet, O God,
overcome by your might and
majesty. You are the greatest!

Amen.

Serve God

Know the God of your
father and serve him with a
whole heart and with a
willing mind.

1 Chronicles 28:9 esv

STRAIGHT TALK

When they call to me, I will answer them; I will be with them in trouble, I will rescue them and honor them.

PSALM 91:15 NRSV

When Bill Moyers was a special assistant to President Lyndon Johnson, he was asked to say  a prayer at a dinner held at the White House for visiting dignitaries. Moyers began his prayer by speaking softly to God. President Johnson, sitting several seats away at a long table, said, "Speak up, Bill. I can't hear you." Moyers, an ordained minister, stopped in midsentence and without looking up, said, "But Mr. President, I wasn't addressing you." He was addressing God.

When you pray, talk directly and specifically to God. Tell him how it is with you, how you want it to be, and how he can help you. Talk to him from your heart.

When talking to God, speak clearly, boldly, and expectantly.

Call on Me in the day of trouble;
I will deliver you, and you shall
honor and glorify Me.

PSALM 50:15 AMP

God, thank you for hearing
me whether I talk to you
silently or aloud.

Amen.

PUT IN PERSPECTIVE

A thousand years in your sight are but as yesterday when it is past, or as a watch in the night.

PSALM 90:4 ESV

A wealthy man listened intently to the sermon and then invited a young minister to have  lunch with him at his vast estate after the worship service one Sunday.

After a gourmet dinner facilitated by servants, the rich man invited the minister out on his veranda. "Something you said in your sermon bothered me," he told the minister. "You said everything belonged to God. But look at all that," he said as he pointed to his fields, barns, and livestock. "I have worked hard many years for all that. It belongs to me, doesn't it?" The minister, wise beyond his years, responded, "Ask me that question one hundred years from now."

Put things in perspective by acknowledging that everything belongs to God.

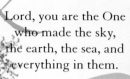

Lord, you are the One
who made the sky,
the earth, the sea, and
everything in them.

ACTS 4:24 NCV

Dear God, when I look to
you, the direction is always up.

Amen.

> *Through [Christ] you believe in God, who*
> *raised him from the dead and glorified him,*
> *and so your faith and hope are in God.*
>
> 1 PETER 1:21 NIV

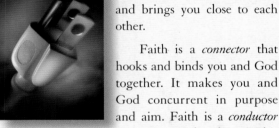

Faith is a relationship between God and you. Faith aligns you with God and brings you close to each other.

Faith is a *connector* that hooks and binds you and God together. It makes you and God concurrent in purpose and aim. Faith is a *conductor* that takes your petitions to God and carries his power to you. It makes possible conversation and communication between you and God. Faith is a *conveyor* that brings God to you and brings you to God. Through faith, you and God are brought into each other's presence. In that presence, you can take God at the word he speaks to you.

Faith opens the eyes of your soul to the quality of your relationship with God.

To have faith is to be sure of the
things we hope for, to be certain
of the things we cannot see.

HEBREWS 11:1 GNT

Dear God, it is by hope that I
long for your presence and by
faith that I come into it.

Amen.

AN OPEN DOOR

I assure you, most solemnly I tell you,
that I Myself am the Door for the sheep.
JOHN 10:7 AMP

In the construction of the usual wooden door there are four panels separated by a long upright center board and a shorter horizontal board. These two boards form the pattern of a cross. This long utilized plan for making doors came from a carpenters' guild in England in the Middle Ages. The artisans in that guild worked the sign of the cross into every door they made. It is no surprise that the motto of this particular carpenters' guild was the words Jesus spoke to the people in Jerusalem: "I am the Door."

As a carpenter and craftsman, Jesus understood the importance of doors. He knew that doors give people access.

Jesus is the door through which you enter God's will and are at home there.

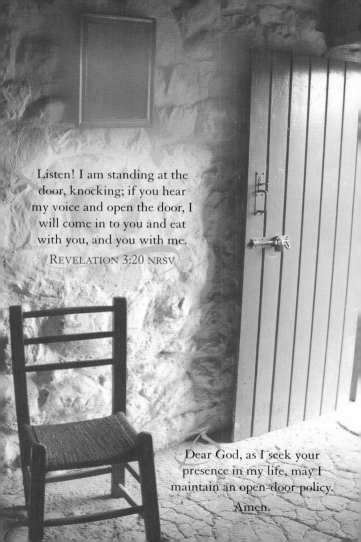

Listen! I am standing at the door, knocking; if you hear my voice and open the door, I will come in to you and eat with you, and you with me.

REVELATION 3:20 NRSV

Dear God, as I seek your presence in my life, may I maintain an open-door policy.

Amen.

IT TAKES TIME

I pray to you, Lord. So when the time is right,
answer me and help me with your wonderful love.

PSALM 69:13 CEV

Quiet moments in God's presence may need scheduling. Put your time with God on your calendar and stamp it non-negotiable. When someone asks you to do something that conflicts with that time, say, "Sorry, I already have an appointment." Have respect for what you set aside for God. Understand it as holy time.

Meeting God is about time. It is about understanding minutes and hours, and knowing what *daily* means. It is about labeling your time "God" and defending your choice against all competitors. It takes time to pray and meditate. It takes time to remember and reflect. It takes time to know God as he can be known.

Time is an irretrievable resource. Plan your time wisely. Use it prudently. Spend it with God.

Go into the city to a certain man and tell him, "The Teacher says: My appointed time is near. I am going to celebrate the Passover with my disciples at your house."

MATTHEW 26:18 NIV

Dear God, my time is in your hands. Put your presence in my heart.

Amen.

YOUR TIME IS NOW

This is the day that the LORD has made.
Let us rejoice and be glad today!
PSALM 118:24 NCV

The past and the future are good places to

visit, but you live in the present. This minute is a rich gift God puts in front of you. See it gratefully, and enter it expectantly. This minute is filled with potential. The minute before you right now invites you to meaningful
movement, fervent hope, and forthright effort. It is, for you, a golden opportunity.

Be good at now. It is God's gift, and it is your time. Use the past to inform and correct; regard the future with hope and vision; live in the now. There is no greater power than to live in the present tense.

Live more fully in the present. Receive the present as the great and rich blessing it is.

You know how to interpret
the appearance of earth and
sky, but why do you not
know how to interpret the
present time?

LUKE 12:56 ESV

Dear God, thank you for the
gift of now. Lead me to fruitful
action in the present moment.

Amen.

GROW SLOWLY

Some seeds fell in good soil, and the plants sprouted, grew, and bore grain: some had thirty grains, others sixty, and others one hundred.

MARK 4:8 GNT

Don't be in a hurry with spiritual life. Slow down and let God have his way with you. It takes time to be deep, rich, and full. That which grows slowly becomes strong. It perseveres and endures, from bud to blossom to fruit.

It takes time to know when, where, and how God speaks. In your life with God, take the time to hear what God is saying to you, where he wants you to be, and what he wants you to do. Take the time to understand how God makes his will known. Spiritual growth is a process that occurs little by little, step by step.

God is a long-range planner. It takes time to get to where God wants you to be.

I will drive them out before
you little by little, until you
become fruitful and take
possession of the land.

EXODUS 23:30 NASB

Dear God, by your plan and
power I grow toward the
goals you set for me.

Amen.

HELP GOD GROW YOU

I planted, Apollos watered,
but God gave the growth.
1 CORINTHIANS 3:6 NRSV

God needs help in growing your spiritual life. Paul and Apollos understood this. They  knew that they planted and watered but God gave the growth. What they put in the ground, God brought forth from the ground. What they nurtured, God flourished.

When speaking of spiritual growth, the images of acorn and oak are often used. It is certainly true that small acorns become large oak trees. You, however, unlike acorns, can choose to enable or to inhibit your growth. You enable it by the choices you make, the goals you set, and the self-discipline you practice. Determined intentionality is a key to growing your spiritual life.

Knowing God is like mining for gold. You have to do some digging.

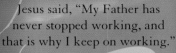

Jesus said, "My Father has never stopped working, and that is why I keep on working."

JOHN 5:17 CEV

Dear God, whatever I can do to deepen my life in you is a great and rich blessing.

Amen.

KNOWING WHOM TO THANK

That night the secret was revealed to Daniel in a vision. Then Daniel praised the God of heaven, saying, "Praise the name of God forever and ever, for he alone has all wisdom and power."

DANIEL 2:19–20 NLT

Time spent with God is praise time for God's good gifts. Raise your praise to the God of your blessings, benefits, and bounty. Alone with God, take the opportunity to tell how much what he does on your behalf means to you. Take what's in your heart, put it on your lips, and tell God how great he is in your life.

The magic words you learned as a child, *Thank you,* are just as important in your relationship with God as they are in your relationships with other people. When you give thanks to God, you acknowledge what wonderful gifts he has given you.

The most significant prayer you will ever pray is just two words long: "Thank you."

Every good gift and every perfect gift is from above, and comes down from the Father of lights, with whom there is no variation or shadow of turning.

JAMES 1:17 NKJV

Dear God, I praise you for all the good things you give me.

Amen.

ON YOUR SIDE

*If anyone sins, we have an Advocate with
the Father, Jesus Christ the righteous.*

1 JOHN 2:1 NASB

When the Bible says God is your advocate, that means that God is on your side. His love for you is so great that he always comes out in favor of you. God puts his big mark of love and encouragement next to your name every time. You can count on God's backing and advocacy.

God's belief in you is your assurance and stability throughout the ups and downs of your days. Knowing God is on your side, you can tackle each challenge with confidence and can persevere toward your goals. God's love for you and faith in you is a support system on which you can depend no matter what happens.

Wherever you go today, God is at your side and on your side.

Make glad the soul of Your servant, for to You, O Lord, I lift up my soul. For You, Lord, are good, and ready to forgive, and abundant in lovingkindness to all who call upon You.

PSALM 86:4–5 NASB

Dear God, thank you for thinking I am special. May I think as much of myself as you think of me.

Amen.

A ANY OTHER NAME

God said to Moses, "I AM WHO I AM." He said further, "Thus you shall say to the Israelites, 'I AM has sent me to you.'"

EXODUS 3:14 NRSV

There is one God with many names. He has many names because there are many ways he wants to help you. For instance, when you need God's healing touch, call on *Jehovah-Rapha*, "the Lord your healer." When you are confused about something, call on *Jehovah-Shalom*, "the Lord your peace."

When you are short of energy or your finances are in bad shape, call on *Jehovah-Jireh*, "the Lord your provider." When you lack direction and don't know which way to turn, call on *Jehovah-Raah*, "the Lord your caring shepherd." When you are down in the dumps and can't get excited about anything, call on *Jehovah-Nissi*, "the Lord your banner."

No matter what name you use, God is your God. Call on him. He is on call for you.

Abraham planted a tamarisk
tree in Beersheba and worshiped
GOD there, praying to the
Eternal God.

GENESIS 21:33 THE MESSAGE

Dear God, you have a name I
can call on for everything I need.

Amen.

A HEART FOR GOD

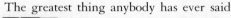

May He grant you according to your heart's desire, and fulfill all your purpose.

PSALM 20:4 NKJV

The greatest thing anybody has ever said about David is that he had a heart for God. His heart was committed to God and filled with love for him. God ruled David's life from his heart. When David wanted to know what to do, he listened to his heart. When David wanted to feel close to God, he looked inside his heart.

Make your heart a place for God. Fill it to full and running over with God's love for you and God's will for you. Invite God into your heart to direct your steps and inspire your life.

You can have a heart for God; a heart is where God belongs, where he will always find a home.

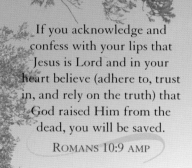

If you acknowledge and
confess with your lips that
Jesus is Lord and in your
heart believe (adhere to, trust
in, and rely on the truth) that
God raised Him from the
dead, you will be saved.

ROMANS 10:9 AMP

Dear God, come into my heart
and make it your home.

Amen.

YOU KNOW

If you only knew the gift God has for you and who I am,
you would ask me, and I would give you living water.

JOHN 4:10 NLT

The world, in all its varied and lavish beauty, says that God loves you. Your own life, with its possibilities and blessings, indicates the source of the great love you are given. The story of God coming to earth in Jesus Christ paints a conclusive picture of God's love.

Jesus sat on the edge of a well one day and talked to a woman about the gift of God's love for her. She didn't understand at first, but after a while she came to know that it was God who loved her. "If you only knew," Jesus had said. Now, beyond doubt or speculation, she knew.

God gives conclusive evidence of his love for you. It is all around you everywhere.

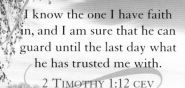

I know the one I have faith
in, and I am sure that he can
guard until the last day what
he has trusted me with.

2 TIMOTHY 1:12 CEV

Dear God, thank you for all
the ways I know that you love
me with an everlasting love.

Amen.

TUNING AND TRAINING

*Their delight is in the law of the LORD, and
on his law they meditate day and night.*
PSALM 1:2 NRSV

The purpose of meditation is to attune your
spirit to God and what he wants you to do in the

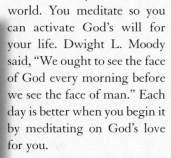

world. You meditate so you
can activate God's will for
your life. Dwight L. Moody
said, "We ought to see the face
of God every morning before
we see the face of man." Each
day is better when you begin it
by meditating on God's love
for you.

The Bible says that before
Mary accepted her role in the life of Jesus, she
pondered the words of the angel in her heart.
She rolled them over in her heart, prayerfully
considering each one. She meditated on them.

Meditation is concentrating on one thing. It
calls you to sit awhile in front of a word from
God.

Let the words of my mouth and the meditation of my heart be acceptable in Your sight, O LORD, my rock and my Redeemer.

PSALM 19:14 NASB

Dear God, I will listen long enough to hear and look far enough to see. Amen.

Know God

Grow in grace and understanding of our Master and Savior, Jesus Christ. Glory to the Master, now and forever! Yes!

2 PETER 3:18 THE MESSAGE

WHAT GOD IS DOING IN YOUR LIFE

He who calls you is faithful; he will surely do it.

1 THESSALONIANS 5:24 ESV

Quiet time is a good time to see more clearly what God is doing in your life. With interference shut down and interruption shut  out, the fog of busyness lifts and you see what God is about on your behalf. Without people and issues to claim your time and attention, you can look beyond the immediate scene to the larger picture of how God is moving in your life to fulfill his will for you.

See his action in your daily events; see his purpose in the happenings of every day. What previously confused becomes clear to you. You understand what God is doing and how he is doing it.

God is doing good things in your life. Look around and see what they are.

God is able to make all grace abound to you, so that in all things at all times, having all that you need, you will abound in every good work.

2 Corinthians 9:8 niv

Dear God, thank you for working behind the scenes to help me perform your will on the stage of my life.

Amen.

WHAT YOU CAN DO

If any want to become my followers, let them deny themselves and take up their cross and follow me.

MATTHEW 16:24 NRSV

Finding leads to following. When you find the ways in which God is working in your life,  pay attention and follow his lead. Where is he leading you? In your quiet moments, consider the shape that God's purpose is taking in your mind and heart. Seek to fulfill that purpose with who you are, what you do, and where you're going.

A man stopped at a traffic light behind another car. While waiting for the light to change, he noticed a bumper sticker on the car in front of him. It read, *Are you following Jesus this close?* That's a good question, isn't it? What would your answer be?

Just as important as experiencing God is what results from that experience.

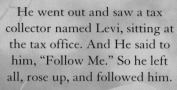

He went out and saw a tax collector named Levi, sitting at the tax office. And He said to him, "Follow Me." So he left all, rose up, and followed him.

LUKE 5:27–28 NKJV

Dear God, help me to do *with* my life what you are doing *in* my life.

Amen.

HOLD ON TO GOD

Hear my cry, O God; attend to my prayer. From the end of the earth I will cry to You, when my heart is overwhelmed; lead me to the rock that is higher than I.

PSALM 61:1–2 NKJV

The psalmist David felt overwhelmed about something that happened in his life, but he still celebrated God as his high and secure rock. He experienced God as a refuge and shelter. David had many images to paint a picture of how God protected him in the midst of trouble and kept him safe when danger came near.

David may have come to the end of his rope, but he hung on to the knot of security and steadfastness God had tied there. He understood the place of his power and the source of his strength.

When you hold on to God, you are holding on to someone that won't let you go. To get a hold on yourself, hold on to God.

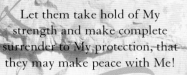

Let them take hold of My
strength and make complete
surrender to My protection, that
they may make peace with Me!

Isaiah 27:5 amp

Dear God, no matter what happens
to me, I know without a doubt that
I can depend on you.

Amen.

THINK IT OVER

*Our LORD, I will remember the things you
have done, your miracles of long ago. I will
think about each one of your mighty deeds.*

PSALM 77:11–12 CEV

A Chinese philosopher insisted on riding
his mule backward so he would not be dis-
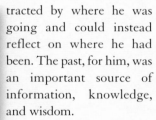
tracted by where he was
going and could instead
reflect on where he had
been. The past, for him, was
an important source of
information, knowledge,
and wisdom.

Where you have been
holds important and significant meaning for the
present and for the future. When you evaluate
the past, you see its teaching and learn its lessons.
When you value the past, you acquire its power.
Adlai Stevenson said, "You can chart your
future clearly and wisely only when you know
the path which has led to the present."

Your quiet moments with God give you a
chance to mull over the meaning and purpose of
what has already taken place.

I remember you while I'm
lying in bed; I think about
you through the night. You
are my help. Because of your
protection, I sing.

PSALM 63:6–7 NCV

Dear God, I turn back to
understand how you have
blessed me day after day.

Amen.

CONSIDER IT AGAIN

This book of the law shall not depart from your mouth,
but you shall meditate on it day and night, so that you
may be careful to do according to all that is written in it.
JOSHUA 1:8 NASB

To contemplate something is to consider it until you understand it. For instance, when you sit quietly in a garden for a long time and watch a butterfly move among the flowers, you come to understand the beauty, grace, and purpose of butterflies.

Or if a builder stands in front of large piles of rocks studying their size and shape, he or she begins to get an image of a grand cathedral. You see what you look at over and over. Repetition leads to insight and knowledge. You come to know in your heart what you consider in your mind. You come to recognize in your will what you contemplate in your heart.

There are great lessons in contemplating what has happened and pondering why it has happened.

The Spirit will give him wisdom and understanding,
guidance and power. The
Spirit will teach him to know
and respect the LORD.

ISAIAH 11:2 NCV

Dear God, I will consider
again and again the counsel
and direction you give me.

Amen.

FULL OF SURPRISES

What no one ever saw or heard, what no one ever thought could happen, is the very thing God prepared for those who love him.

1 CORINTHIANS 2:9 GNT

Raymond Miller came across a set of old long-handled forks and thought they would be  good to roast marshmallows with his children. Just like his grandmother had done with him, he thought. That night, as he scrubbed the forks and rubbed away the grime, he discovered there on the handles, under layers of tarnish, were the initials A.M. The forks had belonged to his grandmother, Amanda Miller.

Something like that occurs when you get close to God. The nineteenth-century mathematician Bernhard Riemann said, "I did not invent those pairs of differential equations. I found them in the world, where God had hidden them."

You discover great truths about God when you get close to him.

The king answered and said to Daniel, "Truly, your God is God of gods and Lord of kings, and a revealer of mysteries, for you have been able to reveal this mystery."

DANIEL 2:47 ESV

Dear God, there is so much about you I look forward to discovering and to knowing.

Amen.

HELP ON THE WAY

GOD is good, a hiding place in tough times. He recognizes and welcomes anyone looking for help.
NAHUM 1:7 THE MESSAGE

During the filming of the movie *Quo Vadis,* there was a scene in which actress Deborrah  Kerr was exposed alone to a whole pride of lions. Afterward she was asked by reporters covering the making of the movie if she had been afraid. With a glint in her eye, she replied, "Oh no, I had read the script and knew that Robert Taylor would come and save me."

When you get into some kind of trouble and call on God for aid, be assured that help is on the way. You can count on it. God comes quickly and promptly to give you assistance. It is God's intention to rescue and deliver you.

No matter where you are when you call on God for help, he hears and comes.

She came and, kneeling,
worshiped Him and kept
praying, Lord, help me!

MATTHEW 15:25 AMP

Dear God of instant help,
thank you for coming to me
any time and every time.

Amen.

ALWAYS MORE

Now we see a dim reflection, as if we were looking into a mirror, but then we shall see clearly. Now I know only a part, but then I will know fully, as God has known me.

1 CORINTHIANS 13:12 NCV

Your eyes are made to take in a wide range of colors that span the spectrum of your consciousness and awareness, from red at one end of the spectrum to violet at the other end. But this is not all the color there is. There is infrared beyond the red and there is ultraviolet beyond the violet. Your eyes are not made for these colors but they are there all the same.

Likewise, there is more to God than you know or understand—great mystery, unparalleled majesty, unspeakable glory, and immeasurable love. Beyond your perceptions and understandings of God, there is God himself.

No matter how much you know about God, there is always more than you perceive or comprehend.

Great indeed, we confess, is the mystery of godliness: He was manifested in the flesh, vindicated by the Spirit, seen by angels, proclaimed among the nations, believed on in the world, taken up in glory.

1 TIMOTHY 3:16 ESV

Dear God, thank you for the ever-expanding glory of who you are to me.

Amen.

JUST DO IT

> *Peter and the other apostles replied:*
> *"We must obey God rather than men!"*
>
> ACTS 5:29 NIV

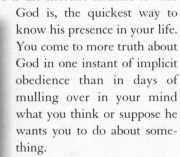

Obedience is the shortest distance to who God is, the quickest way to know his presence in your life. You come to more truth about God in one instant of implicit obedience than in days of mulling over in your mind what you think or suppose he wants you to do about something.

There is no substitute in the Christian life for obedience. It brings the blessing of God's presence and power to you. When you do what God wants, you know God is present within you to make you strong for your life. You are assured of God's strengthening company, and you go forth in confidence.

Obedience opens the door to God's presence and power in your life.

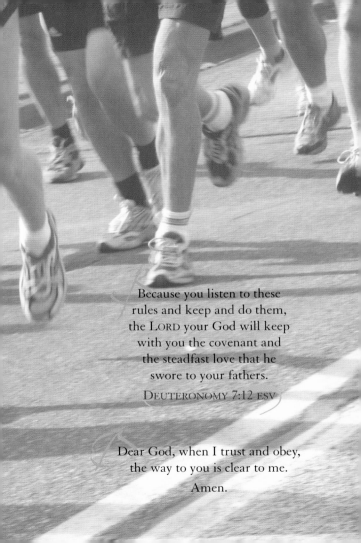

Because you listen to these
rules and keep and do them,
the LORD your God will keep
with you the covenant and
the steadfast love that he
swore to your fathers.

DEUTERONOMY 7:12 ESV

Dear God, when I trust and obey,
the way to you is clear to me.

Amen.

GOD GETS BIGGER

The earth and everything on it belong to the
LORD. The world and its people belong to him.
PSALM 24:1 CEV

The closer you get to God, the better you
see who he is. The better you
see who God is, the more you
realize how big he is. From a
distance, you can only guess
about God's ability. Up close,
you can feel his strength.

In *Prince Caspian,* by C. S.
Lewis, there is a wonderful
conversation between Lucy
and the lion Aslan. Aslan is,
for Lewis, a Christ figure. Lucy looks at Aslan
and says, "You're bigger." Aslan explains why
Lucy thinks he is bigger. "That is because you
are older, little one." Aslan sees that Lucy is confused and finishes the explanation. "Every year
you grow, you will find me bigger."

The closer you get to God, the more you
know of his might and majesty.

Yes, the LORD pours down
his blessings. Our land will
yield its bountiful crops.

PSALM 85:12 NLT

Dear God, I am grateful that
you are big and strong.

Amen.

THIRSTY ENOUGH

On the last day of the festival, the great day, while Jesus was standing there, he cried out, "Let anyone who is thirsty come to me."

JOHN 7:37 NRSV

The central condition for an abundant spiritual life is awareness of your need. Jesus, on the day of a great feast, made this clear. He would provide drink, he said, for those who know and admit they are thirsty. Thirst is the primary and prior condition. God offers the fullness of himself to those who are spiritually thirsty.

Thirst means an awareness of your need and a conscious desire for that need to be met. You need not suffer from unmet needs if you tell God what your needs are and ask him to help you with them. God puts the resources of his power and providence at your disposal.

When you pray because you need help from God, the answer to your prayers is on its way.

When he heard that it was Jesus of Nazareth, he began to cry out and say, "Jesus, Son of David, have mercy on me!"

MARK 10:47 ESV

Dear God, when I bring my needs to you, you give me the help I need.

Amen.

WANTING IT

> *Delight yourself also in the LORD, and He shall give you the desires of your heart.*
> PSALM 37:4 NKJV

Desire is at the heart of spiritual growth. How much do you desire a closeness to God?

How intense are you about discovering and following God's will for you? How high is your desire quotient?

If you want to grow in your spiritual life, want all that God has in store for you. Desire all the love and grace he has stored up for you. Saint Catherine of Siena is credited with saying that "God does not ask a perfect work but only infinite desire." God wants you to want him. God honors this desire for him by coming to you in great and gracious ways.

There's an old spiritual that says, "Lord, I want to be a Christian in my heart." "Want to be" is the key.

Some of you keep competing for
so-called "important" parts. But
now I want to lay out a far
better way for you.

1 CORINTHIANS 12:31 THE MESSAGE

Dear God, I desire with all my
heart that you come to me in
every way that you will.

Amen.

SLEEP WELL

I will allow no sleep to my eyes, no slumber to my eyelids, till I find a place for the LORD, a dwelling for the Mighty One of Jacob.

PSALM 132:4–5 NIV

Conrad had been sleeping better in the past few weeks. He no longer tossed, turned, and watched the clock tick slowly on. In the morning, the bedcover didn't look like there'd been a major wrestling match there the night before. Conrad, wondering why it had taken place, told his friend Randy about the improvement.

Randy asked Conrad if any significant changes had occurred in his home life. Was his job any different? Conrad answered no to both questions. Then Randy said, "How about your spiritual life? Are you praying more? Do you feel more of God's love in your heart?" Conrad smiled brightly and nodded knowingly.

When you make positive strides in your spiritual life, you sleep better.

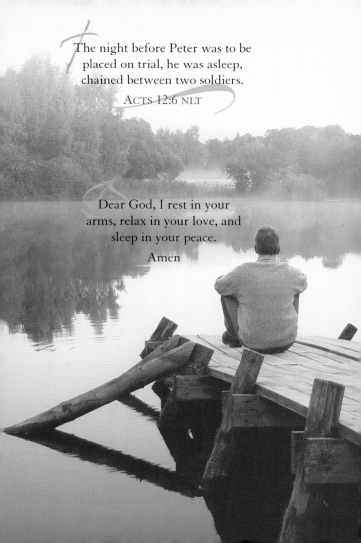

The night before Peter was to be
placed on trial, he was asleep,
chained between two soldiers.

ACTS 12:6 NLT

Dear God, I rest in your
arms, relax in your love, and
sleep in your peace.

Amen

PRACTICE YOUR PRAYERS

The Lord is far from the wicked, but He hears the prayer of the [consistently] righteous.

PROVERBS 15:29 AMP

Out of your prayer life comes a desire to love people. When you talk with God about

yourself, he talks to you about others. He points out whom you are to love and how you are to love.

During World War II, a soldier was by his bunk in the barracks saying his prayers just before taps. Another soldier, bothered by the show of piety, threw his heavy combat boot and hit the praying man on the head, knocking him down. The first soldier said nothing. The other soldier laughed and went to bed, forgetting to retrieve his boot. The next morning, he found both of his boots by his bed, beautifully spit-shined. The two soldiers ended up praying together.

Talking to God sends you out to love other people.

The LORD is near to all who call upon Him, to all who call upon Him in truth.

PSALM 145:18 NKJV

Dear God, as I speak to you, speak to me about those you want me love today.

Amen.

Believe God

To all who believed
him and accepted him,
he gave the right to
become children of God.

JOHN 1:12 NLT

A FOREVER CHILD

Very truly, I tell you, whoever believes has eternal life.
JOHN 6:47 NRSV

When you let God into your heart, you belong to him forever. An unbreakable relation-ship has been established. When the great scientist Michael Faraday lay dying, a friend asked him, "What are your speculations about what is to come?" Faraday replied, "I have no speculations. I rest my soul on certainties." When you make God yours, it is certain you will be forever his.

Over the main door to the Cathedral of Milan are three mottos. The left panel of the door reads, "All that pleases is but for a moment." The right panel reads, "All that troubles is but for a moment." The central panel reads, "All that matters is forever."

Nothing can untie the knot of your eternal condition.

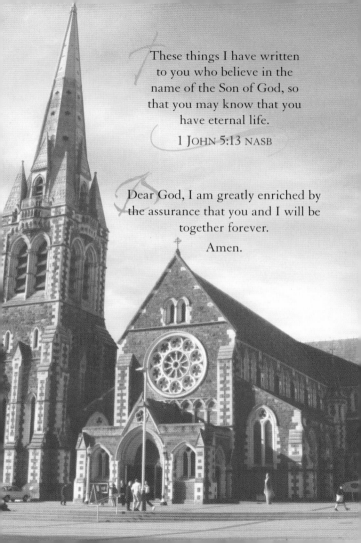

These things I have written to you who believe in the name of the Son of God, so that you may know that you have eternal life.

1 JOHN 5:13 NASB

Dear God, I am greatly enriched by the assurance that you and I will be together forever.

Amen.

GOD CALLS YOU

If any of you want to come with me, you must forget yourself, carry your cross, and follow me.

MATTHEW 16:24 GNT

Saint Francis of Assisi turned his back on wealth and inheritance to follow God. One day

he discarded his clothes and walked naked and alone out of the city. Along the way, he saw a leper sitting on the side of the road. At first he passed the leper by, but he then went back to where he sat and embraced the diseased man.

Francis continued on his journey but, after a few steps, looked back to see the leper one last time. No one was there. Saint Francis believed that the leper was Jesus Christ and that through that event God called him to a life of service on behalf of others.

God calls you to be with other people and to love them in his name.

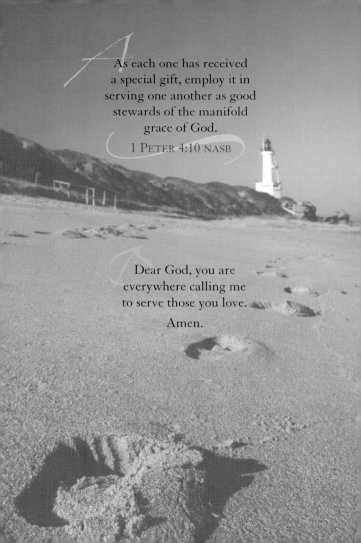

As each one has received
a special gift, employ it in
serving one another as good
stewards of the manifold
grace of God.

1 PETER 4:10 NASB

Dear God, you are
everywhere calling me
to serve those you love.

Amen.

WHERE GOD IS

As the mountains surround Jerusalem, so the LORD
surrounds his people both now and forevermore.

PSALM 125:2 NIV

A will once filed in Murphy, North
Carolina, created a puzzling
situation. An eccentric woman
had left a large part of her
estate to God. In order to settle
the matter, a lawsuit was filed
naming God as the defendant.
The local sheriff was appointed to serve the summons on
the defendant. Several weeks
later, he turned in the follow-
ing report: "After due and diligent search, I
have concluded that God cannot be found in
Cherokee County."

God leaves evidence of himself all around.
He writes his name on the garments of nature.
He sends his love through generous and gracious friends. He fills the church with the warm
spirit of his presence.

God makes himself known to you in many
ways and in many places.

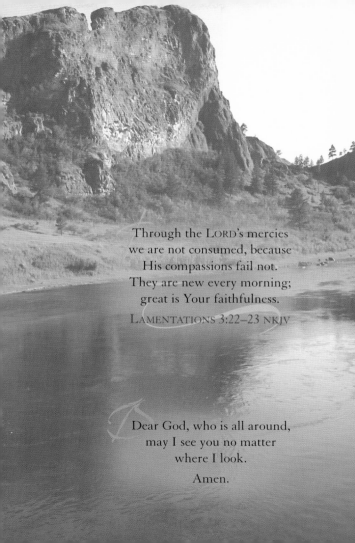

Through the LORD's mercies
we are not consumed, because
His compassions fail not.
They are new every morning;
great is Your faithfulness.

LAMENTATIONS 3:22–23 NKJV

Dear God, who is all around,
may I see you no matter
where I look.

Amen.

WHAT GOD IS DOING IN YOUR WORLD

I am the vine, and you are the branches. Those who remain in me, and I in them, will bear much fruit; for you can do nothing without me.

JOHN 15:5 GNT

Your challenge each day is to find out what God is doing in the part of the world where you live and join him in doing whatever that is. How can your personal thoughts and actions, even attitudes, relate to the activity of God? How is God moving today in the place where you are?

You know what God is doing by looking around you for evidence of his activity. You see God involved in institutions that care for people. He is obvious in causes that promote good values and strong principles. Be aware of where God is working, and join him there.

Discern the divine in everyday life, and join forces with God in what he is doing. Give yourself to God's work.

God has made us what we are. In Christ Jesus, God made us to do good works, which God planned in advance for us to live our lives doing.

Ephesians 2:10 ncv

Dear God, show me what you are doing so I can help accomplish your will in the world.

Amen.

MADE LIKE GOD

God created humankind in his image, in the image of
God he created them; male and female he created them.
GENESIS 1:27 NRSV

When sixteen-year-old Dan entered an elevator in a department store, a woman stared at him, looking him over from head to toe. She made Dan nervous. After looking at him three or four times, the woman explained the reason for her scrutiny. She said to him, "You're Eric's boy, aren't you?" She recognized him from knowing his dad.

You are made in the image of God and resemble your maker. You have inherited God's essential qualities of love and joy. You have within you characteristics that speak of God's passion and faithfulness. Who you are has the print of God all over it.

You are made in the image of God. You come from God. You are unmistakably his.

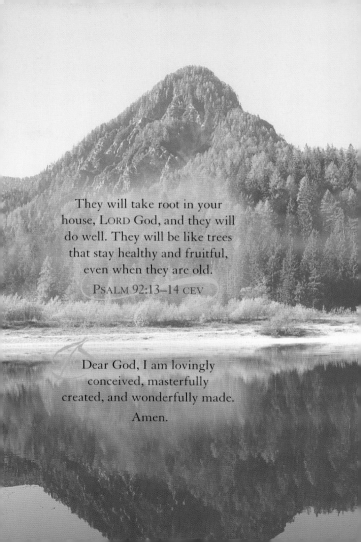

They will take root in your house, LORD God, and they will do well. They will be like trees that stay healthy and fruitful, even when they are old.

PSALM 92:13–14 CEV

Dear God, I am lovingly conceived, masterfully created, and wonderfully made.

Amen.

FREE TO LOVE GOD

Seek the LORD and His strength; seek His face evermore! Remember His marvelous works which He has done, His wonders, and the judgments of His mouth.

1 CHRONICLES 16:11–12 NKJV

In C. S. Lewis's *The Screwtape Letters,* Screwtape says to his nephew Wormwood that he cannot understand why God does not take away the will of those who do not choose to follow him. Screwtape talks about two weapons he knows God has, the Irresistible and the Indisputable, and ponders why they are never used. If God used these weapons, his creation would have to follow him in all things.

God could have programmed you to do his will. Instead, he made you free to say yes or no to him. When you say yes, you love God because you want to—not because you have to.

You are free to love God. Loving God is your choice and your privilege.

I will study your teachings and
follow your footsteps. I will
take pleasure in your laws and
remember your words.

PSALM 119:15–16 CEV

Dear God, you honor me
with the freedom to love
and serve you.

Amen.

GET IT RIGHT

> *A new commandment I give to you, that you love one another; just as I have loved you, you also are to love one another.*
>
> JOHN 13:34 ESV

A pastor called to a new church preached his first sermon on loving one another. It was an excellently crafted and well-delivered sermon. The congregation responded enthusiastically to the sermon, and everyone looked forward to the following Sunday when the new pastor would preach again.

The following Sunday, the pastor again preached well, but it was exactly the same sermon. And on the third Sunday his sermon was identical to the previous two. The governing board of the church was quite concerned and asked the pastor when he would go on to preach on another topic. Without hesitation, he replied, "As soon as we get this one right."

God wants you to love other people. Keep working on that until you get it right.

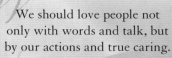

We should love people not
only with words and talk, but
by our actions and true caring.

1 JOHN 3:18 NCV

Dear God, thank you for loving
me day in and day out. Help me
to love others in the same way
that you love me.

Amen.

YOUR FATHER

The time is coming when the true worshipers will worship the Father in spirit and truth, and that time is here already. You see, the Father too is actively seeking such people to worship him.

JOHN 4:23 NCV

In the entire Old Testament God is referred to as Father only six times, and then not very personally. But in the Gospels, Jesus speaks of God as "my Father" or "our Father" more than sixty times. When Jesus came to earth, he reversed the traditional concept of God. God is no longer removed and remote. There is every reason for you to refer to him as your Father.

There is something very concrete, nothing abstract, about talking to God your Father. It's a sit-down, face-to-face, close-enough-to-touch kind of thing. Talking to God as your Father is the most intimate of conversations.

When you talk to God your Father, you speak with someone you know and someone who knows you.

When Jesus had spoken these
things, He lifted up His eyes
to heaven and said, Father,
the hour has come.

JOHN 17:1 AMP

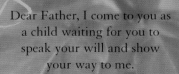

Dear Father, I come to you as
a child waiting for you to
speak your will and show
your way to me.

Amen.

GOD IS GREAT

The LORD your God is supreme over all gods and over all powers. He is great and mighty, and he is to be obeyed.

DEUTERONOMY 10:17 GNT

If you close down interferences and interruptions to be alone with God, nothing detracts you from God. He is in front of you. He alone is there.

At the funeral of Louis XIV, the light of many candles, symbolizing the brightness and greatness of the king, filled the room. At the appointed time, the court preacher stood to address those who had come to honor the king. He nodded his head toward several attendants, who in turn snuffed out every one of the candles. The cathedral was now completely dark. Out of that darkness, the court preacher spoke. "God only is great," he said.

No one is as great as God. Only he creates and sustains the world. Only God has you in the palm of his hand.

God thunders wondrously with his voice; he does great things that we cannot comprehend.

JOB 37:5 NRSV

Good and great God, you are everything to me. You set the stars in place. You live in my heart.

Amen.

HOW YOU LOOK AT IT

*He said to them, "Come, and you will see." So
they came and saw where He was staying; and
they stayed with Him that day.*

JOHN 1:39 NASB

The closer you get to God, the more your perspective about God changes. Through the eyes of reverence, God comes across in a different way. Who he is becomes clearer. It was said of an early-twentieth-century photographer that he had "the ability to see beyond the lens." So also can you.

God is like a prism. What you see depends on how you turn the glass. Turn it in faith and see the greatness of God. Turn it in love and see the warmth of God. Turn it in hope and see the promises of God. Turn it in anticipation and see the guidance of God. Turn it in assurance and see the eternity of God.

The closer you get to God, the more of him you see.

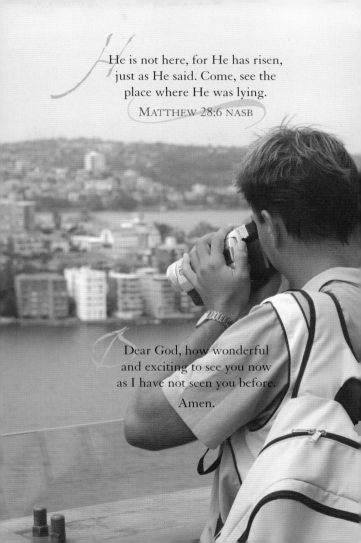

He is not here, for He has risen,
just as He said. Come, see the
place where He was lying.

MATTHEW 28:6 NASB

Dear God, how wonderful
and exciting to see you now
as I have not seen you before.

Amen.

FENCES DOWN

*Faith in Christ Jesus is what makes each of you
equal with each other, whether you are a Jew or a
Greek, a slave or a free person, a man or a woman.*
GALATIANS 3:28 CEV

When you take time and make room to get
close to God, you acquire a
more inclusive attitude
toward other people. You see
that God loves everybody and
wants you to do the same.
Divisions between you and
others melt away before the
bright and warm glow of
God's universal embrace.

A man stood up in church after a terrible
hurricane hit his city and talked about his backyard fence. Ferocious winds had blown it into
splintered fragments and left him exposed to a
neighbor he'd never met. It wasn't long before
they were barbecuing together, a result of taking
time and making room for each other.

Unity is the birthplace of God's purpose
for you. It is where you feel God's love in its
richness.

How wonderful, how beautiful,
when brothers and sisters get along!

PSALM 133:1 THE MESSAGE

Dear God, in your love, my
arms are wide open to other
people. In you, we have
much in common.

Amen.

Follow God

They shall follow my
ordinances and be careful
to observe my statutes.

EZEKIEL 37:24 NRSV

MORE THAN YOU THINK

How sweet are Your words to my taste,
sweeter than honey to my mouth!
PSALM 119:103 NKJV

A faithful churchgoer had to miss the Sunday service one week. On Monday morning, he asked his neighbor for a report on church. He asked questions about the anthem, the Bible reading, the sermon. To each question, she replied, "I don't remember."

"What good did it do for you to go church?" he said. "You don't remember a thing." His neighbor thought about that and then reached down and picked up a wicker basket and asked him to bring her a basket of water. He told her it was impossible to carry water in a wicker basket. "I know it is," she said. "But don't you think the basket would be cleaner afterward?"

Your faithfulness to the priorities of God washes across your heart in love and renewal.

I will sing to the LORD as long as I live; I will sing praise to my God while I have my being.

PSALM 104:33 NASB

Dear God, as I pray to you and praise you, I am transformed and made new.

Amen.

THE WEIGHT OF YOUR WORRY

*The eternal God is your refuge and dwelling place,
and underneath are the everlasting arms; He drove
the enemy before you and thrust them out.*

DEUTERONOMY 33:27 AMP

In an early manuscript of the Christian era, there is a record of a man named Titedios Amerimnos. The first part of that name is a proper name, but the second part is made up of the Greek word for *worry* plus the prefix meaning *never*.

This man is thought to have added the second part of his name after he became a Christian. He was then "Titedios, the man who never worries." A life of worry is on the natural plane, but the Christian life is on a spiritual plane. There is no need to worry when one trusts in God.

Put the weight of your worry on God. Give him your tomorrows, and trust them to his care and wisdom.

Humble yourselves, therefore,
under the mighty hand of God
so that at the proper time he
may exalt you, casting all your
anxieties on him, because he
cares for you.

1 PETER 5:6–7 ESV

Dear God, I will quit wringing
my hands and place them in yours
for you to hold and guide me.

Amen.

HARD-TIMES FAITH

Look at the proud! Their spirit is not right in them, but the righteous live by their faith.
HABAKKUK 2:4 NRSV

The prophet Habakkuk lived in hard times. Babylon was threatening Judah, and God didn't seem to be doing anything about it. Habakkuk asked God to address the problem, and then he waited. At last God spoke. God told Habakkuk that to get through hard times, he had to have faith.

When you have a problem, you probably wish God would ride in on a champion horse and slay your difficulty. "Take away my problem," you plead with God. But removing your problem is not always best for you. God may have something else in mind, because problems bring you opportunities to do and be your best.

Solving problems is not as important as trusting God in the midst of them.

Be alert, stand firm in the faith, be brave, be strong.

1 CORINTHIANS 16:13 GNT

Dear God, thank you for being with me when I need you the most.

Amen.

DON'T BE AFRAID

Jesus spoke to them, saying, "Take heart; it is I. Do not be afraid."
MATTHEW 14:27 ESV

When Rodney was eight years old, he attended a professional football game in a large stadium in a big city with his dad and some of his dad's friends. When they were leaving the stadium, Rodney got separated from the others. When he realized what had happened, tears flooded his face and sobs convulsed his small body. In full-blown panic, he had no idea what to do.

Just then, Rodney spotted his dad running rapidly down a ramp in his direction. As soon as he saw his dad, Rodney was no longer afraid. Now in his forties, Rodney says that's the day he began to understand who God is to him.

Knowing God is near, you are better able to manage your fears. The presence of God encourages an absence of fears.

I am the LORD your God,
who holds your right hand,
and I tell you, "Don't be
afraid. I will help you."

ISAIAH 41:13 NCV

Lord God, quiet the wind and
waves of my anxieties and fears.

Amen.

WHEN IN TROUBLE

*I will call to you whenever trouble strikes,
and you will answer me.*

PSALM 86:7 NLT

A band of ruffians rose up against David, and he was in big trouble. The insurrectionists tried to assassinate him, but the man whose heart resembled God's knew where to go. He went to God. He prayed. His prayer was made in the confidence that God would respond.

When trouble comes to you, you can't tell trouble your schedule is full. But God knows what to do when you have troubles and difficulties. God is on the job, and things are getting better already. When trouble comes to your life, you know where to go. You know whom to ask for help.

When trouble comes, prayer gets simple. Without enough power of your own, you ask for the power of God.

Take my yoke upon you and learn from me, for I am gentle and humble in heart, and you will find rest for your souls.

MATTHEW 11:29 NIV

O Lord God, let your presence be my promise and your power my strength.

Amen.

RAISED UP

If it's an initiation ritual you're after, you've already been through it by submitting to baptism. Going under the water was a burial of your old life; coming up out of it was a resurrection, God raising you from the dead as he did Christ.

COLOSSIANS 2:12 THE MESSAGE

Paul did not speak of a future resurrection. He spoke of the present experience of living a resurrection life. You die to the pain of troubles, and you rise to the life of new opportunity.

During World War II, a London church prepared for a harvest thanksgiving service; in the sanctuary was a sheaf of corn. An enemy air attack destroyed the church before the service could be held. Months passed, spring came, and someone noticed that on the bomb site there were shoots of green. Summer arrived, the shoots grew, and in the fall a flourishing patch of corn grew in the midst of the rubble. Your trust in the resurrected Christ sends you out as one who believes life is stronger than death.

If you have been raised up with Christ, keep seeking the things above, where Christ is.

COLOSSIANS 3:1 NASB

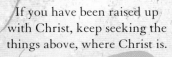

Dear God, thank you for resurrection power in each day, and for its power in the midst of challenge.

Amen.

KNOW WHO KNOCKS

Look at me. I stand at the door. I knock. If you hear me call and open the door, I'll come right in and sit down to supper with you.

REVELATION 3:20 THE MESSAGE

A pastor took money to a woman who was in need of help for herself and her family. He knocked on the door, but there was no answer. He knocked again, more forcefully this time, and no one came to the door. Another day and still another day he repeated his effort, but to no avail.

Eventually, he was able to get the money to her. When he did, she confessed that she had heard him knocking on the door every time he'd been there, but she had thought it was a bill collector. Instead, someone had come to give money to her.

God knocks on the door of your heart to give you gifts of grace and joy.

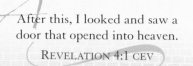

After this, I looked and saw a door that opened into heaven.

REVELATION 4:1 CEV

Dear God, it is you I hear knocking on the door of my heart. I am coming.

Amen.

SOW THE SEED

God is the One who gives seed to the farmer and bread for food. He will give you all the seed you need and make it grow so there will be a great harvest from your goodness.

2 CORINTHIANS 9:10 NCV

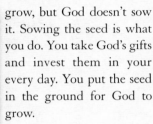

God gives the seed and God makes the seed grow, but God doesn't sow it. Sowing the seed is what you do. You take God's gifts and invest them in your every day. You put the seed in the ground for God to grow.

A woman dreamed of entering a large store in which the gifts of God were kept. Behind one of the counters was an angel dispensing something to those who stood in line. The woman waited her turn and, when it came, said to the angel, "Please give me the fruit I need for my life." The angel responded, "I'm sorry. We don't stock fruit. All we have is seed."

You receive rich possibilities from God and make them richer by what you do with them.

Sow fields and plant vineyards,
and gather a fruitful harvest.

PSALM 107:37 NASB

Dear God, thank you for the
seed you give to me. May I
sow faithfully and wait
expectantly.

Amen.

A SWEET SMELL

*The fig tree forms its early fruit; the
blossoming vines spread their fragrance.*
SONG OF SONGS 2:13 NIV

In California there is a lovely place called
the Valley of Roses. For many miles, lush roses

bloom on both sides of the
road. There are many vari-
eties, and each one is as beautiful and sweet smelling as
the next. They pervade the
air with pleasant scents.
Travelers driving through
the Valley of Roses open the
windows of their cars so they won't miss the full
aroma of the magnificent flowers. The fragrance saturates even the clothes they wear.
When they get home, people know where they
have been from their fragrance.

People know when you have been with
God. When you make the effort to draw close to
God, it is obvious to others.

Time spent with God gives you a sweet fragrance of love, joy, and peace.

He appointed twelve, that they might be with Him and that He might send them out to preach.

MARK 3:14 NKJV

Dear God, as I move through each day, may it be known that I have been with you.

Amen.

HE IS ALIVE

Jesus came and stood among them and said,
"Peace be with you."

JOHN 20:19 NRSV

God raised Jesus from the grave so the spirit and strength of the risen Lord could be with you. He is alive in your relationships and activities. He is available to you in everything you do.

For years, R. W. Dale, an able scholar and a renowned preacher, was a follower of Christ. As he was preparing an Easter sermon for his congregation at Carr's Lane Church in Birmingham, England, the reality of the presence of Jesus swept over him so strongly that he began to pace and shout, "He is alive! He is alive!" Every Sunday thereafter, an Easter hymn was sung in Dale's church. Every Sunday became to him a resurrection day.

Everywhere you go, God goes with you.

Suddenly, Jesus himself came
along and joined them and
began walking beside them.
Luke 24:15 nlt

You are alive, Lord Jesus, in
my heart and in my life. I am
never alone.

Amen.

GOD IS AFTER YOU

This is what the Lord GOD says: I, myself, will
search for my sheep and take care of them.

EZEKIEL 34:11 NCV

You are on God's to-find list. God is after you. He seeks you until he finds you. One person

who understood this was C. S. Lewis. He used a number of metaphors to describe God's relentless pursuit of him.

He likened God to a great angler playing his fish and a cat chasing a mouse. Perhaps Lewis's most remembered metaphor is that of a divine chess player maneuvering him into the most disadvantageous positions until in the end he had to concede. He wrote to a friend who was trying very hard to avoid God in his life, "I think you are already in the meshes of the net. You will not escape."

God wants you. God knows where you are. God is after you. You won't get away.

God understands the way to it, and he knows its place. For he looks to the ends of the earth and sees everything under the heavens.

JOB 28:23–24 ESV

Dear God, thank you for seeking me out no matter where I am or how far that is from you.

Amen.

GOD SENDS YOU

*Go, then, to all peoples everywhere
and make them my disciples.*
MATTHEW 28:19 GNT

It is God's desire that you take love for
him from your heart and put
it into the hearts of other
people.

Years ago, in West
Africa, a man lay on a hospital cot on a suffocatingly
hot day. He had been sick
for a long time and was
extremely weak from the surgery just per-
formed on him. But he was not without hope. In
fact, it surged in his heart. A man in a doctor's
coat stood over him and smiled. It was the man
who had operated on him and saved his life.
"Who sent you?" he asked the doctor. "The
Lord Jesus Christ sent me," answered Albert
Schweitzer.

God has been sending his servants into the
world for a long time. He sends you now.

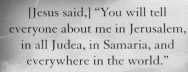

[Jesus said,] "You will tell everyone about me in Jerusalem, in all Judea, in Samaria, and everywhere in the world."

ACTS 1:8 CEV

Dear God, I listen for your call. I am ready to go where you send me.

Amen.

WHAT GOD CAN DO

*I commend you to the care of God and to the
message of his grace, which is able to build you up
and give you the blessings God has for all his people.*
ACTS 20:32 GNT

When you put yourself in God's hands, you
are in a place where great
things can be accomplished in
your life.

Stuart Hamblen was a
radio disc jockey in Los
Angeles in 1949 at the time of
the first large-scale Billy
Graham crusade. Liquor had
come to dominate his life, but after several visits
to crusade meetings, he was converted and lost
his appetite for alcohol. A friend asked, "Have
you not wanted one drink?" Hamblen replied,
"No, John, it is no secret what God can do." His
friend, knowing Hamblen's interest in music,
said, "Stuart, you ought to write a song about
that."

Stuart Hamblen wrote a song about what
God can accomplish in your life. He said it is no
secret what God can do.

244

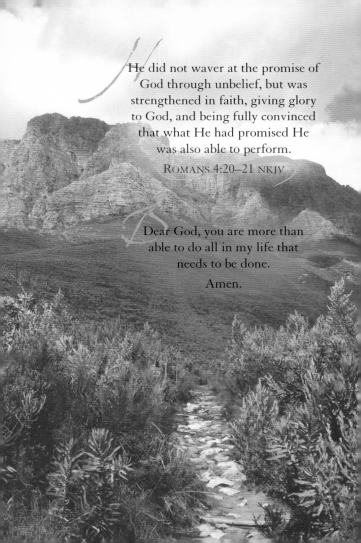

He did not waver at the promise of God through unbelief, but was strengthened in faith, giving glory to God, and being fully convinced that what He had promised He was also able to perform.

ROMANS 4:20–21 NKJV

Dear God, you are more than able to do all in my life that needs to be done.

Amen.

STRAIGHT WITH CROOKED LINES

In all your ways acknowledge him,
and he will make your paths straight.

PROVERBS 3:6 NIV

A young boy had a rough home life and grew up to write books that blessed thousands of

people. A fledgling musician had his violin stolen, found a used trumpet for sale cheap, and became an outstanding band leader. A woman had to drop out of college to care for her mother but later became a doctor because of that experience.

God sometimes uses unlikely means to get to desired ends. He takes something that doesn't look like it would do and makes it work. In his hands, the improbable makes a good outcome possible. God writes straight with crooked lines.

God can see beyond what you can see. He knows what will work in your life better than you do.

I hear the voice of someone shouting, "Make a highway for the LORD through the wilderness. Make a straight, smooth road through the desert for our God."

ISAIAH 40:3 NLT

Dear God, you see beginnings where I see endings, possibilities where I see problems.

Amen.

GOD WASTES NOTHING

Whatever is true, whatever is honorable, whatever is right, whatever is pure, whatever is lovely, whatever is of good repute . . . dwell on these things.

PHILIPPIANS 4:8 NASB

Bad things that happen in your life wake you up to the good stuff you may not otherwise attend to. Problems bring with them an invitation to explore new territory and discover what God has put there for your benefit and the blessing of others.

As a young man, Arturo Toscanini played the cello. His eyesight was poor and he could hardly see the music in front of him, so he had to memorize it. One evening, the orchestra conductor became ill, and Toscanini was the only one who knew the musical score. He conducted the entire program without once referring to the music. His performance was flawless, and his career was underway.

God wastes nothing. He can use anything to bring good to your life.

When you give to them, they gather it up; when you open your hand, they are filled with good things.

PSALM 104:28 NRSV

Dear God, help me look far enough in my life to see the good things you have put there.

Amen.

WHEN YOU STUMBLE

*I, your GOD, have a firm grip on you and
I'm not letting go. I'm telling you, "Don't
panic. I'm right here to help you."*
ISAIAH 41:13 THE MESSAGE

A mother of a toddler watches her child.
When he stumbles and is
about to fall, she reaches out
her hand to catch him. When
he trips over his feet, she
restores his balance. As the
child moves around the room,
she lets him do all he can on his
own. When he falters, she is
there in a flash. She is always
ready to move to his side and give him the assistance he needs.

God gives you that kind of ongoing care
when you invite him into your life. He lets you
walk when you can, but when you get into difficulty, he is there promptly to give you a helping hand.

God has his eye on you. He knows when
you need him to come and help.

The nations of the earth will
walk in its light, and the
rulers of the world will come
and bring their glory to it.

REVELATION 21:24 NLT

Thank you, dear God, for
catching me when I stumble
and putting me upright
when I fall.

Amen.

FOLLOW THE LIGHT

About noon when I came near Damascus, a bright
light from heaven suddenly flashed all around me.

ACTS 22:6 NCV

From the book *Living Love* by Saint
Francis de Sales comes this
story. One day a group of
travelers took a nap under
a large tree. Because the
location was cool and they
were tired, the travelers
slept well.

After a while, the
shade moved and the sun
awakened them. Some of the travelers got up
and resumed their journey. Others turned their
backs on the sun, and went back to sleep. When
they woke up again, night had fallen and they
resumed their journey in the dark. They strayed
in various directions in the forest and soon were
hopelessly lost.

As you draw close to God, you will experience divine light upon your path. When that
light comes, follow it.

God, who said, "Let light shine out of darkness," has shone in our hearts to give the light of the knowledge of the glory of God in the face of Jesus Christ.

2 CORINTHIANS 4:6 ESV

Dear God, may I always follow light that comes from you and is for me.

Amen.

Please God

If you completely obey
these laws, the LORD
your God will be loyal
and keep the agreement
he made with you.

DEUTERONOMY 7:12 CEV

SMALL THINGS COUNT

Having obtained help from God, I stand to this day
testifying both to small and great, stating nothing but
what the Prophets and Moses said was going to take place.

ACTS 26:22 NASB

When God asks you to do something for him, your call might seem small. Often God asks you to do something quite unspectacular, minuscule in scope, and not particularly noteworthy. You want to play first violin, would even be willing to play second violin, but God asks you to pull the curtain.

Pulling the curtain is not at all what you had in mind. Nevertheless, be the best curtain puller you can be. The concert will not go on without you. When the orchestra members are seated and looking spiffy in their tuxedos and gowns, they can't be seen if you don't do your job. The maestro won't mount the podium and conduct the symphony without you.

Give what you have to God. In God's hands nothing is small.

Though your beginning was small, yet your latter end would increase abundantly.

JOB 8:7 NKJV

Dear God, you use whatever I give, and I thank you for recognizing who I am and what I have.

Amen.

GOD CARRIES YOU

He tends his flock like a shepherd; he gathers the
lambs in his arms and carries them close to his heart.
ISAIAH 40:11 NIV

Do you remember what it was like when
you were little and someone
picked you up and carried
you somewhere? What a
comfortable and secure feel-
ing when a parent or an
older sibling reached down
to your small frame, lifted
you into strong and capable
arms, and carted you across
the room or around the yard or up the street. It
was good to be held and carried like that. You
knew everything was okay.

Let God carry you each day. You will feel
safe and secure in the arms of God's compassion
and concern. You will be comfortable everywhere you go because the eternal arms of God's
power and might are underneath you.

You are God's child. God always takes care
of his children.

He took a child and had him stand in front of them. He put his arms around him and said to them, "Whoever welcomes in my name one of these children, welcomes me."

MARK 9:36–37 GNT

Dear God, thank you for supporting me in ways I can feel, know, and trust.

Amen.

HE IS THE POTTER

He used that clay to make another
pot the way he wanted it to be.
JEREMIAH 18:4 NCV

Jeremiah went to the potter's shop one day to watch the potter make pots. He was a good potter and his pots were the most beautiful anywhere around. But something went wrong as the potter worked on a particular vessel. The potter was dissatisfied with the way that vessel looked.

Jeremiah watched what happened next. The potter did not set the unacceptable item aside. He did not throw it away. He took the still soft clay, plied it into a shapeless lump, put it on his wheel, and remolded it until it was beautiful and perfect. Jeremiah then understood how God works in the lives of his people.

God is the potter of your life. You are the clay in his hands. You are the vessel in his heart.

We are the clay, and you are
our potter; we are all the
work of your hand.

ISAIAH 64:8 ESV

Dear God, I am ready and willing
for you to shape me and use me.

Amen.

THE NEW YOU

If anyone is in Christ, there is a new creation: everything old has passed away; see, everything has become new!

2 CORINTHIANS 5:17 NRSV

Shortly after his conversion, Saint Augustine was walking down the street when he met a woman who had been a mistress to him in his rebellious days. He turned abruptly and walked quickly in the other direction. Surprised at his action but thinking he did not recognize her, she cried out to him, "Augustine, it is I!" Augustine, increasing his speed, continued walking away from her and cried back over his shoulder, "Yes, but it is not I."

He meant there was a new Augustine. Since taking God into his life, his actions were different and his behavior had changed. He was not the person he had been. When God comes into your life, he changes and transforms you. You are not the same.

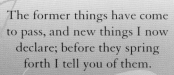

The former things have come
to pass, and new things I now
declare; before they spring
forth I tell you of them.

ISAIAH 42:9 AMP

Thank you, dear God, for
inviting me to change and for
helping me do it.

Amen.

A MASTERPIECE

I'll make you a great nation and bless you.
I'll make you famous; you'll be a blessing.
GENESIS 12:2 THE MESSAGE

During World War II, before the enemy entered Amsterdam, patrons of the arts took the huge paintings of several great masters down  from the walls of a famous museum. They removed the paintings from their frames, rolled them up like rugs, and sealed them in wax to make them waterproof. They moved the priceless paintings through a vast art underground from culvert to granary to farm. This kept the art from falling into enemy hands.

You are God's masterpiece. When God made you, he knew what he was doing, and he did it well. Keep yourself safe from what would deny who you are and to whom you belong. Be vigilant about yourself. You are wonderfully created and superbly endowed. Take good care of what God has made.

You yourselves know how he
has proved his worth, how he
and I, like a son and his
father, have worked together
for the sake of the gospel.

PHILIPPIANS 2:22 GNT

Dear God, I commit myself
to the care of my heart and
the feeding of my soul.

Amen.

WHAT'S ALREADY HAPPENED

I will sing to the Lord, for He has triumphed gloriously; the horse and his rider or its chariot has He thrown into the sea.

EXODUS 15:1 AMP

The children of Israel, beginning with Moses and Miriam, were able to glance into the past and remember their great escape from the Egyptians. Looking to the past, they could document their deliverance. They could recall and rehearse the past from their memory. Knowing God's past mercies allowed them to praise God and to look forward to his continuing presence.

Knowing that God had been with them in the past gave them assurance that he would walk with them in the present and accompany them into the future. They believed he would continue to act on their behalf.

A good memory increases gratitude and assurance. You thank God for what he has done, and you look forward to what he will do.

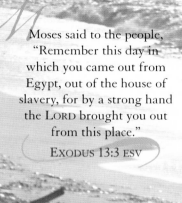

Moses said to the people, "Remember this day in which you came out from Egypt, out of the house of slavery, for by a strong hand the LORD brought you out from this place."

EXODUS 13:3 ESV

Dear God, I remember how you have come time and again to hold and lift me up. Thank you.

Amen.

LIVE WHERE YOU LAND

I have learned how to be content (satisfied to the point where I am not disturbed or disquieted) in whatever state I am.

PHILIPPIANS 4:11 AMP

Years ago, a hot air balloonist was going to make a long trip over a vast area. He planned his itinerary carefully, knowing exactly where he would stop on which day. He took off, confident he would be able to stick to his plan and follow his itinerary.

However, he had not planned adequately for the wind from the mountains. For the first four days, the wind blew him off course. He ended up in towns he'd never been to and didn't know anything about. But in each town where he landed, the hot air balloonist was heard to say, "Had I known about this place I would have planned all along to land here."

Life sometimes takes you off course. Enjoy where you end up. Live where you land.

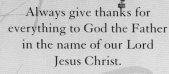

Always give thanks for
everything to God the Father
in the name of our Lord
Jesus Christ.

EPHESIANS 5:20 NLT

Dear God, may I stand in
awe and appreciation before
the surprises of my life.

Amen.

SHOUTING NEWS

Be glad in the LORD and rejoice, O righteous,
and shout for joy, all you upright in heart.

PSALM 32:11 NRSV

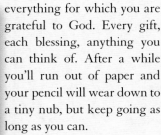

Get a pencil and paper and write down everything for which you are grateful to God. Every gift, each blessing, anything you can think of. After a while you'll run out of paper and your pencil will wear down to a tiny nub, but keep going as long as you can.

Then take your list and, item by item, tell God how much you appreciate what he has done in and through your life. Be excited about your gifts and talents, your abilities and assets. Be exuberant in your praise. Don't hold anything back. Unplug all the stops and let praise pour forth. Your blessings are wonderful news.

Know how much you are blessed, and then show that you know.

There came from the throne the sound of a voice, saying, "Praise our God, all his servants and all people, both great and small, who have reverence for him!"

REVELATION 19:5 GNT

Dear God, when I consider my blessings one by one, I shout to you with exceedingly great joy.

Amen.

WITH UTMOST CONFIDENCE

In Whom, because of our faith in Him, we dare to have the boldness (courage and confidence) of free access (an unreserved approach to God with freedom and without fear).

EPHESIANS 3:12 AMP

You don't have to wait for an invitation to talk to God. You have had a standing invitation since the beginning of time. Just as God made himself available to the couple in Eden's garden on a moment's notice, so also is he available to you.

God is available when things aren't going well in your family. He is available when you are disappointed because you haven't met a goal you set for yourself. God is ready to listen to your every word when someone you care about has let you down or when you have let someone down. Nothing is outside of God's ability and willingness to listen to you and to hear you.

God's door is always wide open. God is always in for you.

We say with confidence,
"The Lord is my helper; I
will not be afraid. What can
man do to me?"

HEBREWS 13:6 NIV

Dear God, I come boldly into
your presence and stand
confidently before your love.

Amen.

FALLING DOWN

Humble yourselves [demote, lower yourselves in your own estimation] under the mighty hand of God, that in due time He may exalt you.

1 PETER 5:6 AMP

The best position from which to see God is on your knees, humbled before God's majesty and magnificence. From your knees you can look up to the greatness and grandeur of God and gain perspective on how splendid and wonderful God is.

Prayer puts you on your knees to receive the fullness of God. Mother Teresa said that prayer "enlarges your heart until it is capable of receiving God's gift of himself." Prayer spoken humbly before God creates many rooms in your heart for God to occupy with his great power and immense love. He comes into those rooms to listen, understand, and speak.

Prayer positions you to receive the gifts of God. It opens your heart to who God is and what God has.

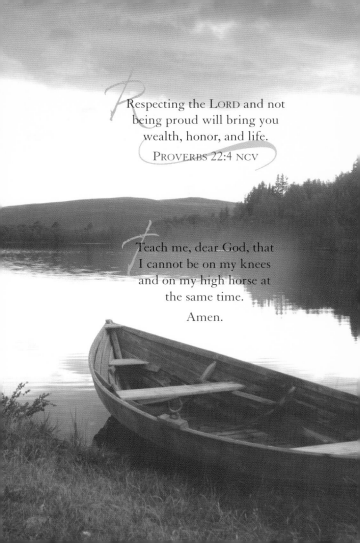

Respecting the LORD and not being proud will bring you wealth, honor, and life.

PROVERBS 22:4 NCV

Teach me, dear God, that I cannot be on my knees and on my high horse at the same time.

Amen.

A THANK-YOU OFFERING

*Through him, then, let us continually offer
a sacrifice of praise to God, that is, the
fruit of lips that confess his name.*

HEBREWS 13:15 NRSV

Your blessings from God make you grate-

ful. The extent and extrava-
gance of God's gifts make
you thankful. When you
acknowledge how good
God is in your life, you let
him know how much you
appreciate what he does for
you. You come before him
in great thanksgiving.

Thanksgiving is the constant and character-
istic note of the Christian life. In happy
moments, praise God. In difficult moments, seek
God. In quiet moments, worship God. In painful
moments, trust God. In every moment, thank
God. As J. B. Lightfoot said, "Thanksgiving is at
the end of all human conduct, whether observed
in words or works."

Giving thanks is the very life of prayer. Tell
God how grateful you are for the fruit that falls
from your tree.

Since we are receiving a kingdom
that cannot be shaken, let us be
thankful, and so worship God
acceptably with reverence and awe.

HEBREWS 12:28 NIV

Dear God, you are the origin
of my blessings and the cause
of my bounty.

Amen.

PEACE SPOKEN HERE

Later on that day, the disciples had gathered together, but, fearful of the Jews, had locked all the doors in the house. Jesus entered, stood among them, and said, "Peace to you."

JOHN 20:19 THE MESSAGE

God's presence brings various gifts to you at different times. There is one gift it always brings: peace. God comes to you as one who calmed the storm of a tumultuous sea, and he puts a holy quiet in a heart committed to him. He silences the noise of conflict and tension.

The Hebrew word for peace is *shalom,* which means "more than enough." God brings you more than enough for your daily walk through life. He gives you more than enough insight to know what to do, more than enough direction to know where to go, more than enough courage to follow the insight and direction you have.

Your God is *Jehovah-Shalom,* "the Lord of peace." He comes to you bearing the gift of peace.

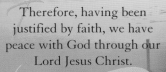

Therefore, having been
justified by faith, we have
peace with God through our
Lord Jesus Christ.

ROMANS 5:1 NKJV

Dear God, thank you for
peace within that does not
depend on happenings. It
depends on you.

Amen.

GIVE GOD THE PIECES

Come to me, all of you who are tired from
carrying heavy loads, and I will give you rest.
                    MATTHEW 11:28 GNT

A sign on the front of a welder's shop said
We weld everything but a broken heart. The sign

on the front of God's love for
you says he can mend even
your broken heart. He can
take the shattered fragments
and restore the wholeness
of your heart in seamless
splendor.

God can take the bits and pieces of
unreached goals and put them together. God
can hold the fragments of what you once
believed about life and make them as new and
fresh as the dawning sun. He can put your hope,
vision, and confidence back together. God can
touch the hole in your heart and fill it with his
love and his grace.

God can mend your broken heart, if you
give him the pieces.

Be humble under God's powerful hand so he will lift you up when the right time comes. Give all your worries to him, because he cares about you.

1 PETER 5:6–7 NCV

Dear God, I come to you with my brokenness. You can make me whole again.

Amen.

THE WONDER INSIDE YOU

God created humankind in his image, in the image of God he created them; male and female he created them.

GENESIS 1:27 NRSV

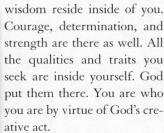

The best side of you is the inside of you. That's where the image of God is. Love, joy, and wisdom reside inside of you. Courage, determination, and strength are there as well. All the qualities and traits you seek are inside yourself. God put them there. You are who you are by virtue of God's creative act.

Draw close to what God has put inside you. Let it show you who you are to God and reveal who God is to you. Let it uncover your purpose, illumine your path, and bring the glow of God's love to all you do. What you need for a purposeful and meaningful life is inside you.

Listen to the inside of you, where God speaks.

Delight yourself also in the
LORD, and He shall give you
the desires of your heart.

PSALM 37:4 NKJV

Dear God, I look within myself to
where you are. I see you there.

Amen.

Obey God

*If you keep My
commandments [if
you continue to obey
My instructions], you
will abide in My love
and live on in it.*

John 15:10 AMP

THE POWER WITHIN YOU

You have already won a big victory over those false teachers, for the Spirit in you is far stronger than anything in the world.

1 JOHN 4:4 THE MESSAGE

Because God made you, there is a great power within you. Hudson Taylor, a nineteenth-century missionary to China, said, "All giants have been weak people who did great things for God because they reckoned on his power within them."

Did you ever buy something that ran on batteries but you didn't know that? You took your purchase out of the bag when you got home, and there it was right in front of your startled eyes: *Batteries not included.* You couldn't use what you bought because it had no source of power. Your personal source of power is God. He brings his strength to your weakness and enables you to rise above what holds you down.

What is before or beyond you fades when approached by what is within you.

I pray that out of [God's] glorious riches
he may strengthen you with power
through his Spirit in your inner being.

EPHESIANS 3:16 NIV

Dear God, let your Spirit
have his way within me.
Guide me and teach me
along the way.

Amen.

A LIFE OF PROCESS

We are to grow up in all aspects into
Him who is the head, even Christ.

EPHESIANS 4:15 NASB

The spiritual life is one of becoming. It is more process than event, and the process is  always going on. The spiritual life is not so much reaching a destination as it is being on the road. You are on the road to a deeper understanding of who God is, to a more personal acceptance of God in your life, and to more joy and love than you have known before.

Whistler, the great painter, once lost a shipment of blank canvasses. A friend asked him if they were of any great value. The master artist pulled on his chin, his eyes twinkled, and he said, "Not yet, not yet."

The spiritual life is one of expansion and extension. There is always room for more.

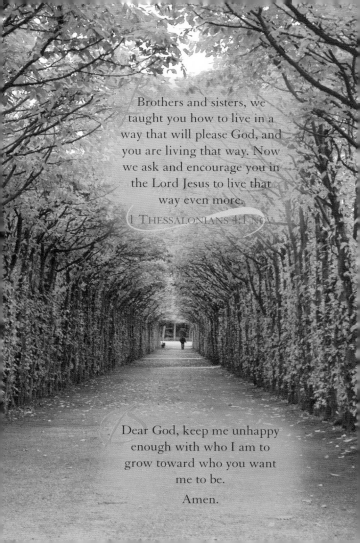

Brothers and sisters, we
taught you how to live in a
way that will please God, and
you are living that way. Now
we ask and encourage you in
the Lord Jesus to live that
way even more.

1 Thessalonians 4:1 NCV

Dear God, keep me unhappy
enough with who I am to
grow toward who you want
me to be.

Amen.

INSIGHT IS BETTER

If any of you lack wisdom, you should pray to God, who will give it to you; because God gives generously and graciously to all.

JAMES 1:5 GNT

Insight is more potent than eyesight. The famous singer Ray Charles had no sight, but he

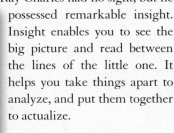

possessed remarkable insight. Insight enables you to see the big picture and read between the lines of the little one. It helps you take things apart to analyze, and put them together to actualize.

Hindsight shows you where you have been and foresight shows where you are going, but insight helps you understand and comprehend all the movements of life. Someone who understood this placed this bumper sticker on her car: *I brake for insights*. Insight occurs when God's wisdom comes to your mind. The gift of God's wisdom makes the path before you both clearer and brighter. You see more, you see better. Insight helps you search within so you can see ahead.

To the one who pleases him
God has given wisdom and
knowledge and joy.

ECCLESIASTES 2:26 ESV

Dear God, thank you for the
insight that enables me to
more closely follow you and
your will for me.

Amen.

COMING IN TO GO OUT

Come, see the place where the Lord lay. And go quickly and tell His disciples that He is risen from the dead, and indeed He is going before you into Galilee.

MATTHEW 28:6–7 NKJV

The spiritual life is a coming in and a going out. When Jesus' friends went to the empty tomb to honor his memory, they were greeted by an angel who told them to *come* into the tomb where Jesus had been placed. Next, he told them to see that Jesus was not in the tomb anymore. Then, they were to *go* from the empty tomb into the world to *tell* the good news of the resurrection of Jesus Christ from the dead. Come in and see, go out and tell.

God wants you to have inward and outward movements. Go inside yourself to be with God, and go out to others to take God to them.

Retreat to the sanctuary, and then advance to the streets where people need God.

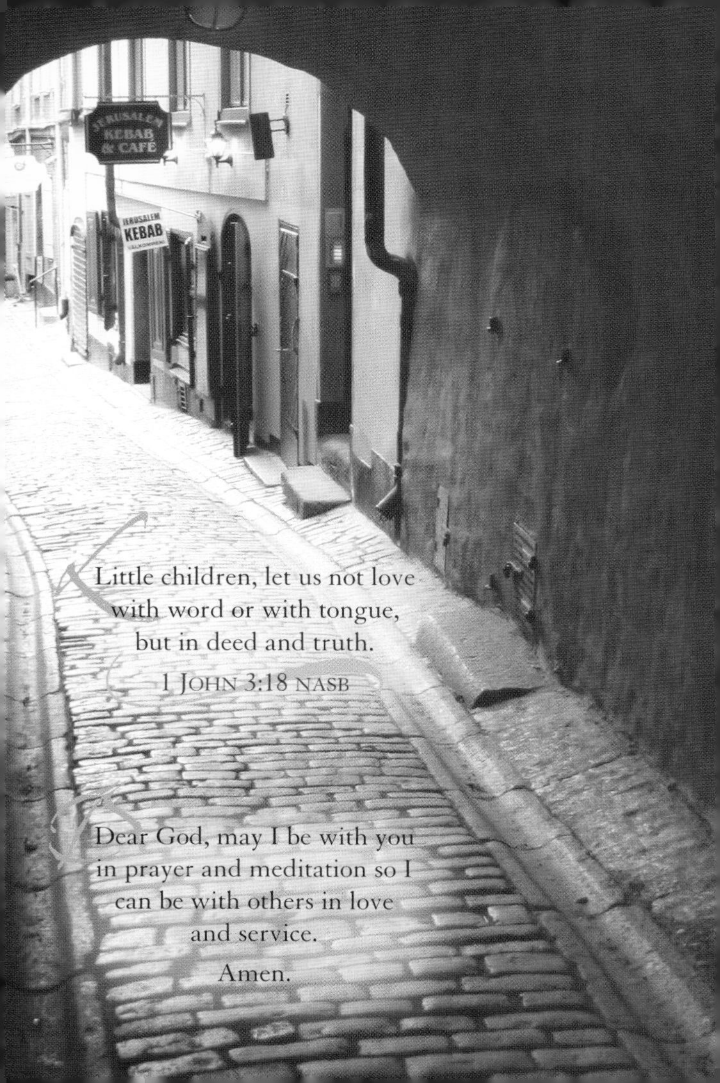

Little children, let us not love
with word or with tongue,
but in deed and truth.

1 JOHN 3:18 NASB

Dear God, may I be with you
in prayer and meditation so I
can be with others in love
and service.

Amen.

SPIRITUALLY CORRECT

Do not conform yourselves to the standards of this world, but let God transform you inwardly by a complete change of your mind.

ROMANS 12:2 GNT

When you are socially correct, you use respectful words to refer to particular people and topics. You conform to a certain standard. When you are spiritually correct, you conform to God's standard. You say and do what God expects you to say and do. There are words and actions that are acceptable and unacceptable to God. There is a prescribed way to conduct yourself as a Christian. As one popular admonition phrases it, "Live so the preacher won't have to lie at your funeral."

Take the high road of word and deed. Be fair to other people. Practice honesty in all your transactions. Hold yourself to the standard God has for you. Follow God's moral compass. Do what is right. Live by God's code of conduct. Be spiritually correct.

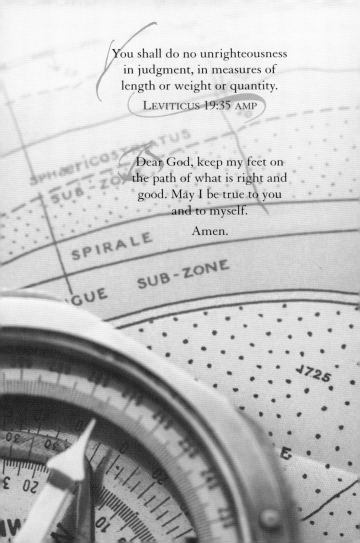

You shall do no unrighteousness
in judgment, in measures of
length or weight or quantity.

LEVITICUS 19:35 AMP

Dear God, keep my feet on
the path of what is right and
good. May I be true to you
and to myself.

Amen.

WHY YOU ARE

> *We are God's workmanship, created in*
> *Christ Jesus to do good works, which God*
> *prepared in advance for us to do.*
>
> EPHESIANS 2:10 NIV

As you spend time in prayer, God talks to you about purpose. He lets you in on why he made you in the first place and what he expects from you now that you are here. God makes known his purpose for you, calls you to devote yourself to that purpose, and promises to help you fulfill it.

God has a rationale for your life that fits his will. He has a reason for your life that pleases him. He has a cause for your life that helps him get his work done. You do not live randomly or aimlessly. You live according to God's purpose for you.

God has something better than a wonderful plan for your life. He has a wonderful purpose for your life.

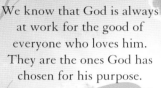

We know that God is always
at work for the good of
everyone who loves him.
They are the ones God has
chosen for his purpose.

ROMANS 8:28 CEV

Dear God, I am grateful for
a purpose in my life that
clearly comes from you.

Amen.

GOD KNOWS THE WAY

I am the way, the truth, and the life. No one can come to the Father except through me.

JOHN 14:6 NLT

Imagine riding on a train through a difficult mountain passage. A lot of things could  happen to the train. At the most it could derail and bring great harm to you. At the least you might be late for an important appointment. But you are not worried because your best friend is the engineer. Everything will be all right because he knows the way to where you are going and knows how to get you there.

When you become friends with God, you develop confidence in him. You have faith that he understands where you need to go and knows how to get you there. God is in charge, and everything is all right.

When you travel with God, don't worry. You won't get lost. God knows the way.

Whether you turn to the right or to the left, your ears will hear a voice behind you, saying, "This is the way; walk in it."

Isaiah 30:21 niv

Dear God, thank you for showing me the way and going with me in it.

Amen.

GOD'S HANDWRITING

The heavens keep telling the wonders of God,
and the skies declare what he has done.

PSALM 19:1 CEV

God has written his name everywhere. But you have to know what you're looking at. A

young man visited the Grand Canyon and had a picture of himself taken on one of the famous ridges. He was proud of the picture, and he took it home to show his mother. She looked at it but didn't say a word about the Grand Canyon. Instead, she told her son she liked the new shoes he had on in the picture and asked where he had bought them.

When you look for God's signature and know that is what you are doing, you will see it everywhere. Every place and every person exhibits the handwriting of God.

Wherever you look, you see the handwriting of God. His name is everywhere.

He shall come down like rain
upon the grass before mowing,
like showers that water the earth.

PSALM 72:6 NKJV

Dear God, everywhere I look
I see evidence that you have
been there.

Amen.

JOY PROVES IT

I have told you these things, that My joy and delight may be in you, and that your joy and gladness may be of full measure and complete and overflowing.

JOHN 15:11 AMP

Joy in your life indicates you belong to God. The Queen of England's standard flies over Buckingham Palace as a sign that the queen is in residence there. Similarly, the joy you show and share is evidence that God lives in your heart. Someone asked Joseph Haydn, the famous composer, why his music was so cheerful. He replied, "I cannot make it otherwise. When I think upon God, my heart is so full of joy that the notes dance and leap from my pen."

Joy is an infallible and undeniable sign of the presence of God in your life. It indicates you have a relationship with God founded on faith and nurtured in love.

Joy in your life leaves no doubt about whom you belong to.

Light is sown for the righteous, and joy for the upright
in heart. Rejoice in the LORD,
O you righteous, and give
thanks to his holy name!

PSALM 97:11–12 ESV

Dear God, I celebrate a life lived
in the joy of your presence and
the pleasure of your company.

Amen.

THEY GO TOGETHER

Blessed are those who have learned to acclaim you,
who walk in the light of your presence, O LORD.
They rejoice in your name all day long; they exult
in your righteousness.

PSALM 89:15–16 NIV

Martin Luther believed the Reformation would be complete when everyone had two things in their possession. He wanted everyone to have a Bible in his or her own language and a hymnal filled with songs of praise and worship. He believed the Bible leads you to a deeper understanding of your faith, and a hymnal enables you to express with great joy the depth and reach of that faith.

Faith and joy go together in your spiritual life. Faith leads you to God, and joy indicates you are glad to be there. Faith reveals how much God loves you, and joy celebrates what that means to you.

Faith says you belong to God. Joy proves you are grateful you do.

It is through faith that all of
you are God's children in
union with Christ Jesus.

GALATIANS 3:26 GNT

Dear God, faith puts you in
my heart and joy lets the
world know you are there.

Amen.

LAUGH OUT LOUD

We laughed, we sang, we couldn't believe our
good fortune. We were the talk of the nations.
PSALM 126:2 THE MESSAGE

Laughter is a precious gift that comes to you from heaven. Laughter is God reaching down to you with delight and gladness. Laughter is a wonderful blessing from God.

God gives laughter because it is good for you. It treats you kindly with healing, wellness, and wholeness. An old Jewish proverb says, "When you are hurt, laugh." Good side-shaking laughter can transform pessimistic diagnosis into hopeful prognosis. It is cheaper and quicker to laugh aloud than to reach into the medicine cabinet or check in to the hospital. Maybe it's a laugh a day rather than an apple a day that keeps the doctor away.

If you laugh a lot, when you get older, your wrinkles will be in all the right places.

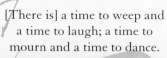

[There is] a time to weep and
a time to laugh; a time to
mourn and a time to dance.

ECCLESIASTES 3:4 NASB

Dear God, thank you for giving
me so many reasons to laugh. I
hear the angels in heaven
laughing with me.

Amen.

WHAT IT MEANS

God, who is rich in mercy, out of the great love with which he loved us even when we were dead through our trespasses, made us alive together with Christ.

EPHESIANS 2:4–5 NRSV

Think about what it means for God to love you. Think about God in heaven loving you enough to make you the unique and wonderful person you are. Think about God coming to earth as Jesus Christ so he could get close enough to love you even more. Think about God loving you to such a degree that he walks with you every step you take in life.

God's love for you is just plain wonderful, isn't it? Nothing can bring you greater joy than the conviction that God loves you. Don't lose sight of that truth. Pound it into your mind and heart every day.

The foundation of faith is God's love for you. God's love for you always comes first.

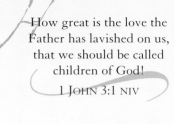

How great is the love the
Father has lavished on us,
that we should be called
children of God!

1 JOHN 3:1 NIV

Dear God, thank you for loving
me more than I can understand
or comprehend.

Amen.

A RESTING FAITH

The fundamental fact of existence is that this trust in God, this faith, is the firm foundation under everything that makes life worth living.

HEBREWS 11:1 THE MESSAGE

Many years ago, a famous evangelist made a distinction between types of faith. He said there are basically three kinds of faith. There is *struggling faith*, which he likened to someone thrashing around in deep water. There is *clinging faith*, which he compared to a person hanging on to the side of a boat. The third kind is *resting faith*, which finds a person safe and secure inside the boat.

Resting faith is the kind of faith God wants you to have. He wants you to trust his presence and depend on his power. He wants you to give yourself completely over to his love and care.

Your faith in God puts you safely into the arms of God. There is no better place to be.

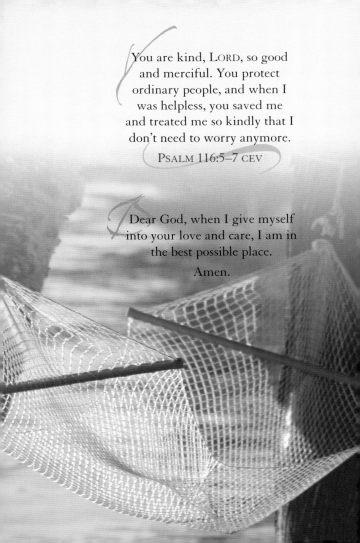

You are kind, LORD, so good
and merciful. You protect
ordinary people, and when I
was helpless, you saved me
and treated me so kindly that I
don't need to worry anymore.

PSALM 116:5–7 CEV

Dear God, when I give myself
into your love and care, I am in
the best possible place.

Amen.

MEETING JESUS

Some Greeks had gone to Jerusalem to worship during Passover. Philip from Bethsaida in Galilee was there too. So they went to him and said, "Sir, we would like to meet Jesus."

JOHN 12:20–21 CEV

Some Greek philosophers came one day to a celebration in Jerusalem. They sought out one of Jesus' close associates and requested to meet with Jesus. They knew about Socrates, but they wanted to see Jesus. They knew about Aristotle and about Plato, but they wanted to see Jesus. They knew about Homer, but they wanted to see Jesus. They believed Jesus was who they truly needed in their lives.

You, too, will have no greater encounter than a meeting with Jesus. No coming together with anybody else measures up. Think of the celebrity you'd most like to meet, and compare that to meeting Jesus. There is no comparison. When you are ready to meet Jesus, he is ready to meet you.

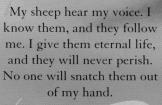

My sheep hear my voice. I
know them, and they follow
me. I give them eternal life,
and they will never perish.
No one will snatch them out
of my hand.

JOHN 10:27–28 NRSV

Lord Jesus, I will meet you
today in many places. You
will be there with me.

Amen.

Remember God

[Jesus said,] "This is my
body given for you; do this
in remembrance of me."

LUKE 22:19 NIV.

YOU KNOW THE NAME

To the church of God which is at Corinth, to those who are sanctified in Christ Jesus, called to be saints, with all who in every place call on the name of Jesus Christ our Lord.

1 CORINTHIANS 1:2 NKJV

A woman sat behind the driver on a sightseeing bus in the Detroit area. "On the right is the Dodge mansion," said the driver. "John Dodge?" inquired the woman. "No, Horace Dodge." A minute later, the driver said, "The house on the left is the Ford home." The woman asked, "Henry Ford?" The driver replied, "No, Edsel Ford."

Another few blocks and the driver called out, "On the left is Christ Church, the largest church in the city." After a couple of minutes, a passenger nudged the woman and said, "Go ahead, lady, you can't be wrong all the time." You can count on the name of Jesus. The name of Jesus in your life brings purpose, power, and peace.

Through [Jesus], therefore, let us constantly and at all times offer up to God a sacrifice of praise, which is the fruit of lips that thankfully acknowledge and confess and glorify His name.

HEBREWS 13:15 AMP

Dear God, thank you for the name of Jesus in my heart and in my life. There is no greater name.

Amen.

WATCH JESUS PRAY

I pray for these followers, but I am also praying for all those who will believe in me because of their teaching.

JOHN 17:20 NCV

As you develop your own prayer life, consider the prayer life of Jesus. The Bible records the words of five of Jesus' prayers and shows him praying on nineteen different occasions. Jesus called on the power of prayer for what God wanted him to say and do.

Jesus began his day in prayer. When you begin your day in prayer, you get it started in the right direction. You connect to God as a power source for your daily encounters and experiences. You take God with you into your relationships and transactions. Starting your day in prayer is the best way to have a good one.

Jesus began his ministry at the Jordan with prayer and ended it on the cross with prayer.

You will call upon me and
come and pray to me, and I
will listen to you. You will seek
me and find me when you seek
me with all your heart.

JEREMIAH 29:12–13 NIV

Dear God, as I watch Jesus
pray I learn how to talk to you.

Amen.

MORE ABOUT JESUS

Then we will be mature, just as Christ is,
and we will be completely like him.

EPHESIANS 4:13 CEV

A wonderful old hymn—"More About Jesus Would I Know"— sings its way into your heart and invites you to grow and mature in your relationship with Jesus. Its words speak of advancement, escalation, and increase.

The time you spend with God provides an opportunity to develop your spiritual life. It invites you forward to larger places of understanding and awareness. Time spent with God is time well spent because it shows you more of who God is and what God can do in your life. Time spent with God brings you closer to him and him nearer to you.

The largest room in your spiritual life and journey is the room for improvement in your relationship with God.

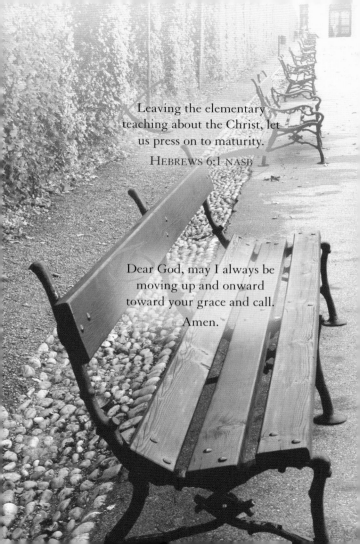

Leaving the elementary
teaching about the Christ, let
us press on to maturity.

HEBREWS 6:1 NASB

Dear God, may I always be
moving up and onward
toward your grace and call.

Amen.

SOUND OF SANDALED FEET

*Suddenly, Jesus himself came along and joined
them and began walking beside them.*

LUKE 24:15 NLT

Jesus pulled up next to people and walked
with them. He did it with
Matthew at the tax office,
Peter and his fishing
partners along the sea,
the women from Galilee
who worked and trav-
eled on his behalf. He
walked with Zacchaeus
to his house for supper. After Jesus was raised
from the dead, he put his stride next to two people walking from Jerusalem to Emmaus. They
heard the sound of sandaled feet.

You know Jesus' presence when you give
him permission to live in your heart. You know
he is there to begin and end each day with you.
You are aware of his touch in all aspects of your
life.

Jesus came into history and stayed. He is
with you now.

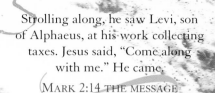

Strolling along, he saw Levi, son
of Alphaeus, at his work collecting
taxes. Jesus said, "Come along
with me." He came.

MARK 2:14 THE MESSAGE

Dear God, you are always
ready to come and make
your presence known to me.

Amen.

GO HIS WAY

Jesus said to him, "Go your way; your faith has made you well." And immediately he recovered his sight and followed him on the way.

MARK 10:52 ESV

Jesus told the previously blind Bartimaeus  to get on his way. Go home, get back to where you were. Bartimaeus didn't go home. He went with Jesus. That's because he understood that Jesus' way was also his way. He knew that when he was with Jesus he was truly at home. Having felt God's healing touch on his eyes, he used his sight to see where Jesus was going so he could follow him there.

You belong with Jesus. That is where you are most at home. That is where life makes more sense, agendas are clearer, power and strength more available. The best way for you to go is the way of Jesus.

When you go the way of Jesus, everything is brighter and better.

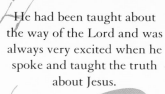

He had been taught about the way of the Lord and was always very excited when he spoke and taught the truth about Jesus.

ACTS 18:25 NCV

Dear God, open my ears so I may hear when you come near to lead me in your way.

Amen.

MEMORIAL

ALWAYS REMEMBER

Think of the wonderful works he has done, the miracles and the judgments he handed down.

PSALM 105:5 NLT

A good way to deepen your spiritual life is to remember when you felt especially close to  God. Keep your mountaintop experiences with God fixed clearly in your mind and planted deeply in your heart. They will renew your faith and refresh your commitment.

When Blaise Pascal died, a friend found a piece of paper sewn into the lining of a jacket the great saint and scientist had worn. On it was scribbled a description of a night when he perceived the fire of God had come down to him. He had never told anyone about that extraordinary night, but with each crinkle of the paper he remembered the glory of it.

You always have with you the memory and reminder of the work of God in your life.

You shall remember that you were a slave in the land of Egypt, and the LORD your God redeemed you.

DEUTERONOMY 15:15 NKJV

Dear God, thank you for all the times you came to me in your presence and power. I remember them well.

Amen.

MORE THAN BAND-AIDS

Sing for joy to God, our strength;
shout out loud to the God of Jacob.

PSALM 81:1 NCV

A college basketball team was having its best season ever. Halfway into its schedule, the team was undefeated and ranked number one in the country. Although some of their games had been close, no one expected their next opponent to be much of a threat. The number-one team was a twenty-point favorite, but their unheralded opponent defeated them by thirty points. "It had been coming," the coach said in a post-game interview. "We've been putting a lot of Band-Aids on our deficiencies."

When you seek God's presence in your life, you don't put Band-Aids on your deficiencies. Through his power, you are made strong.

God makes you strong enough to face life confidently and live it successfully.

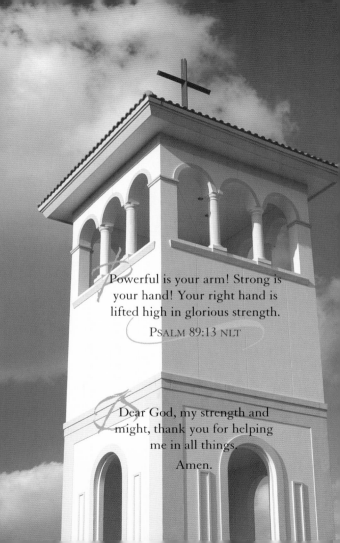

Powerful is your arm! Strong is
your hand! Your right hand is
lifted high in glorious strength.

PSALM 89:13 NLT

Dear God, my strength and
might, thank you for helping
me in all things.

Amen.

JESUS PRAYS FOR YOU

He is always living to make petition to God and intercede with Him and intervene for them.

HEBREWS 7:25 AMP

Close your eyes and imagine Jesus on his knees praying for you. His lips move, and it is

your name he speaks. He talks about your tasks, relationships, and needs. He knows who you are. Jesus prays that your sickness will be healed, your hurt assuaged, and your brokenness mended.

As he prays for you, Jesus commends your desire and compliments your effort. He applauds your accomplishments and achievements. He speaks of your dreams and asks that you have the courage to pursue them. Jesus sets his heart on what is best for you and prays that you be immensely blessed.

The Bible says praying for you is so important to Jesus that he lives in order to do it.

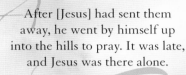

After [Jesus] had sent them
away, he went by himself up
into the hills to pray. It was late,
and Jesus was there alone.

MATTHEW 14:23 NCV

Nothing strengthens me more, dear
God, than to perceive that Jesus is
on his knees praying for me.

Amen.

UNDER SAME MANAGEMENT

Jesus Christ is the same yesterday, today, and forever.
HEBREWS 13:8 NLT

Spending time with God underlines his constancy in your life. When you meet God on a regular basis, you feel the  strong thread of his presence weaving itself through the fabric of your efforts and endeavors. Your sense of his being with you and for you does not come and go. It comes and stays.

God's constancy enables you to make good decisions because you know you can count on his help with what you decide. It gives you courage of conviction because you are assured God will be with you as you respond to what you believe. With God at your side, you have a lifelong supply of confidence.

God never goes away. He is with you to stay.

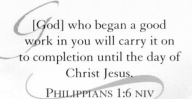

[God] who began a good
work in you will carry it on
to completion until the day of
Christ Jesus.

PHILIPPIANS 1:6 NIV

Dear God, you are my constant
companion. You are with me all
the time everywhere I am.

Amen.

SAFE AT HOME

You faithfully answer our prayers with awesome deeds, O God our savior. You are the hope of everyone on earth, even those who sail on distant seas.

PSALM 65:5 NLT

When children play tag, one of them is "it" and the others in the game try to avoid being tagged by that particular person. The pursuer gives the pursued a certain amount of time for a head start, and then sets out to tag as many people as is possible. When tagged, you have to go and sit on the sidelines. You are out of the game. To counter that predicament, there is a place somewhere in the play area called "home base." When children reach that place, they cannot be tagged. In that place, they are safe.

Your prayer life is a place where you are at home with God. It is a place where God loves and holds you.

Time spent with God in prayer and meditation creates a safe home base.

O Lord, you alone are my hope. I've trusted you, O LORD, from childhood.

PSALM 71:5 NLT

Dear God, when I am close to you I am secure in your love and safe in your care.

Amen.

IN THE BOOK

Their delight is in the law of the LORD, and
on his law they meditate day and night.

PSALM 1:2 NRSV

In 1981 *Chariots of Fire* won the Academy
Award for the best motion picture of the year. A

 few years earlier, a movie
producer had rented a fur-
nished house and was rum-
maging for something to
read. The only book he
could find was *The Official
History of the Olympics.* He
pulled it off the shelf and
began to read. When he came upon a story
about a gifted, dedicated runner who had won a
gold medal in 1924, he knew he had found an
idea for a great movie.

In the time you spend quietly with God, go
to the Bible, where you will find God's defining
word for you.

The Bible is filled with truth about how to
live. You find in it what you need for life.

The statutes of the LORD are
right, rejoicing the heart; the
commandment of the LORD
is pure, enlightening the eyes.

PSALM 19:8 NKJV

Dear God, thank you for
what I hear about myself
when I read your holy Word.

Amen.

WHAT FAITH SEES

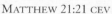

[Jesus said,] "If you have faith and don't doubt, I promise that you can do what I did to this tree. And you will be able to do even more. You can tell this mountain to get up and jump into the sea, and it will."

MATTHEW 21:21 CEV

Faith helps you see more than you think you can. Faith makes you a visionary. It puts concepts and precepts in your mind by which you can build your life beyond what you thought possible. Faith enables you to look farther than you can see and see more than you thought you could.

By faith, Thomas Edison saw light in the darkness. By faith, the Wright brothers saw a way for humans to fly. By faith, Martin Luther King Jr. saw a road to freedom and equality that was hidden to others. By faith, you stare up the steps until you have the courage to step up the stairs.

What you see in your mind and heart is what you get in your life.

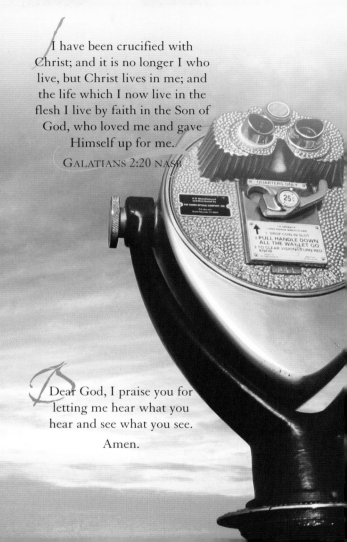

I have been crucified with Christ; and it is no longer I who live, but Christ lives in me; and the life which I now live in the flesh I live by faith in the Son of God, who loved me and gave Himself up for me.

GALATIANS 2:20 NASB

Dear God, I praise you for letting me hear what you hear and see what you see.

Amen.

FOLLOW THE LEADER

*You are blessed, because you see with
your eyes and hear with your ears.*

MATTHEW 13:16 NCV

Several years ago, an advertisement showed
a symphony orchestra with the eyes of every

musician focused on the
conductor. No one was
looking anywhere else.
The caption on the
advertisement said: "The
eternal importance of a
leader." The advertising
company was selling a

series of books on management and wanted to
make an impression about the importance of
leadership.

Your quiet time with God helps you keep
your eyes on Jesus. You can see more clearly in
him your call and purpose. You can take from
him cues and signs that direct you to God's will
for your life. Jesus is your leader. Follow him
closely.

When your eyes are on Jesus, you know
where to go and what to do.

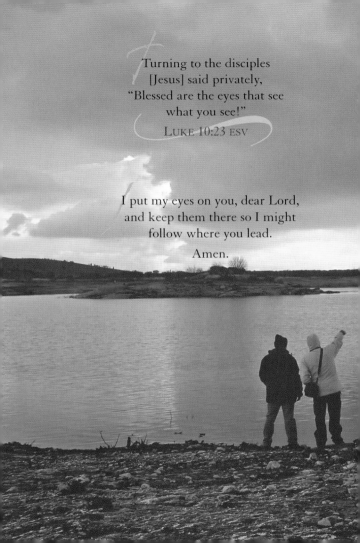

Turning to the disciples
[Jesus] said privately,
"Blessed are the eyes that see
what you see!"

LUKE 10:23 ESV

I put my eyes on you, dear Lord,
and keep them there so I might
follow where you lead.

Amen.

OPEN EVERY DOOR

[Pray] that God will open up to us a door for the word,
so that we may speak forth the mystery of Christ.

COLOSSIANS 4:3 NASB

Listen for the knock of opportunity on the door of life. God sends opportunity because he

loves you and wants the best for you. You are his child and he will provide you with occasions to do well. He has many wonderful places for you to be and he will provide you the means to get to them.

Open every door on which you hear a knock because behind each door is a fresh possibility. Wayne Gretzky, the great hockey player, said that "you miss one hundred percent of the shots you don't take." The best way to live your life fully is to be ready, when opportunity knocks, to open the door and enter the room.

God sends opportunity to knock on your door.

I have set before you an open door, and no one can shut it.

REVELATION 3:8 NKJV

Dear God, when you open a door, no room is small. Thank you for all my opportunities.

Amen.

Need God

God blesses those who
realize their need for him,
for the Kingdom of
Heaven is given to them.

MATTHEW 5:3 NLT

WATCH FOR SIGNS

You wisely and tenderly lead me, and then you bless me.
PSALM 73:24 THE MESSAGE

Downhill skiing is safer when the skier stays on the designated trail. To leave the trail is  to risk danger and flirt with disaster. Snow drifts, icy spots, and fallen trees can cause harm to the skier. Because of these threats, signs are posted on the trail that warn skiers not to go beyond certain boundaries. The signs make clear where the skier ought to be at all times.

When you draw close to God, he makes known where you ought to be in your life. He gives you signs that warn of pitfalls and perils. He tells you about temptations and enticements you should avoid. He shows you how to stay on the path of his will for you.

When you stay on God's path, he keeps you safe.

From now on every road you
travel will take you to GOD.
Follow the Covenant signs;
read the charted directions.

PSALM 25:10 THE MESSAGE

Dear God, thank you for the
path you put before me and
the signs you place on it.

Amen.

GET YOUR FAITH LIFTED

*When Jesus heard this, he was astonished and said
to those following him, "I tell you the truth, I have
not found anyone in Israel with such great faith."*

MATTHEW 8:10 NIV

When Jesus commended the soldier for his
great trust, he was making a
faith comparison. By applaud-
ing the military commander for
believing his servant could be
healed, Jesus was saying some
people have more faith than
others. To increase your faith,
spend time with God and draw
close to him.

The important thing in faith development
is not to compare where you are to others but to
compare it with yourself. Where are you now in
comparison to where you were before? Is your
faith being lifted to a higher level? In your faith,
be superior to your previous self. In your
Christian life, have a faith that regularly increases and steadily rises.

Your faith increases as you focus more and
more on who God is to you.

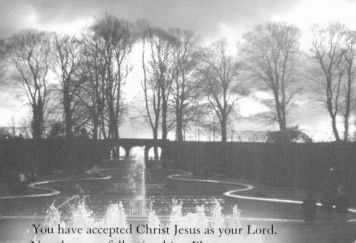

You have accepted Christ Jesus as your Lord.
Now keep on following him. Plant your roots
in Christ and let him be the foundation for your
life. Be strong in your faith, just as you were
taught. And be grateful.

COLOSSIANS 2:6–7 CEV

Dear God, thank you that I
do not have to stay where I
am in my faith. I can go
deeper and rise higher.

Amen.

WHO HAS IT

I enjoy pleasing you. Your Law is in my heart.

PSALM 40:8 CEV

A basketball in your hands is worth a few dollars. In Michael Jordan's hands, it was worth  millions. A tennis racket could possibly be useless in your hands, but in Pete Sampras's hands it was worth a Wimbledon championship. Talent makes all the difference.

In ancient times, a rod was a piece of wood used as a cane or staff, but in Moses' hands it parted the Red Sea and delivered the children of Israel toward the Promised Land. Moses understood this because he spent time at the burning bush drawing close to God. He learned what God can do with talents and skills when they are given to him.

God multiplies and magnifies what you give to him of yourself.

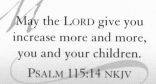

May the LORD give you
increase more and more,
you and your children.

PSALM 115:14 NKJV

Dear God, thank you for
knowing what to do with
what I give you.

Amen.

SURRENDER ALL

I trust in you, O LORD; I say, "You are my God."
My times are in your hand; deliver me from the
hand of my enemies and persecutors.

PSALM 31:14–15 NRSV

Give your problems, challenges, and difficulties to God, but make sure there are no claw marks on them. The

great missionary Jim Elliot once prayed, "Father, let me lose the tension of the grasping hand." Give God your situations willingly, without disclaimer or condition. Without reservation, give God your relationships, employment issues, and inner struggles. Give God all your choices and say to him, "It's your call."

Turn things over to God. He knows better what to do with them than you do. Let God carry you. He is better able to do that than you. It is letting go, not holding on, that makes you strong. It is coming to God with full hands and leaving with empty ones. Give control to God. Make him Lord of your life.

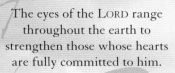

The eyes of the LORD range
throughout the earth to
strengthen those whose hearts
are fully committed to him.

2 CHRONICLES 16:9 NIV

Dear God, thank you for
receiving what I bring and
giving what I need.

Amen.

PRAYER POWER

Confess your sins to one another and pray for one another, so that you will be healed. The prayer of a good person has a powerful effect.

JAMES 5:16 GNT

Prayer changes things. Prayer has power. When John Knox got on his knees to pray, the queen feared his prayers more than she did all the armies of Scotland. When John Wesley prayed, life-changing renewal came to England. When Jonathan Edwards said his fervent prayers, a great revival spread throughout the American colonies. Over and over, history records the power of prayer.

Your prayers have power. God works through praying people. He makes his way known to those who submit themselves prayerfully to him. He accomplishes his purposes through those who offer their urgent and sincere prayers to him. God sends your prayers out with power to affect, change, and bless.

The Lord is far from the wicked, but He hears the prayer of the [consistently] righteous.

PROVERBS 15:29 AMP

Dear God, I believe that you give your power to my prayers.

Amen.

MOVE FORWARD

I run straight toward the goal in order to win the prize, which is God's call through Christ Jesus to the life above.

PHILIPPIANS 3:14 GNT

God accepts and loves you as you are, but he

doesn't want you to stay there. God is interested in your moving forward to new places of opportunity and influence. He wants you to see what you are able to accomplish for his kingdom and for his people. He equips you with what you need to accomplish that to which he calls you.

Someone asked David Livingstone where he was prepared to go, and he replied, "Anywhere, as long as it is forward." He understood that the Christian life is one of forward movement on behalf of what God wants done in the world. Walk toward the dreams, visions, and goals God puts before you.

God invites you to walk through open doors that lead to large rooms.

He was looking forward to the
city that has foundations, whose
designer and builder is God.

Hebrews 11:10 esv

Dear God, in the same way that Jesus walked
out ahead of his disciples on the way to
Jerusalem, I see where you are in my life.

Amen.

OPEN TO GOD

I am the LORD your God, who brought you up out of the land of Egypt. Open your mouth wide and I will fill it.

PSALM 81:10 NRSV

When you spend time with God seeking his will in your life and his way for your life, you are  like a baby bird standing before its parent with mouth wide open, wanting to be fed. You are hungry for the nourishment and sustenance of God's Word.

You want to partake of his grace that comes in the assurance of his love for you. You desire to be filled with the promise of God's direction and the power of his guidance. You want his mercy and forgiveness to be in your heart, wash away your sin, and heal your regret. You are hungry for all that God has for you. You don't want to miss any of it.

Your heart is open to God's great and gracious blessings.

You'll feast on my fresh-baked
bread spread with butter and
rock-pure honey.

PSALM 81:16 THE MESSAGE

Dear God, when I come to
you to be fed, I never go
away hungry. It's always
a feast.

Amen.

THE CHALLENGE OF IT ALL

*Because the Sovereign LORD helps me, I will not
be disgraced. Therefore have I set my face like
flint, and I know I will not be put to shame.*

ISAIAH 50:7 NIV

Leave your comfort
zone and move out into new
territory on behalf of God's
kingdom. You grow in
Christ when you do some-
thing for God beyond what
you've already mastered. You
sense God's presence with
you in personal and intimate
ways.

When you attempt something difficult for
God, you discover God's resources. For instance,
if you make a witness speech in church even
though that makes you uncomfortable, you discover abilities previously unknown to you.
Commitment and effort precede awareness of
talents and skills. It is not necessary to wait until
you think you are ready to do something for
God. Do it, and God will make you ready.

Commit your way to the Lord . . . ; trust (lean on, rely on, and be confident) also in Him and He will bring it to pass. And He will make your uprightness and right standing with God go forth as the light, and your justice and right as [the shining sun of] the noonday.

PSALM 37:5–6 AMP

Dear God, disturb me when I am too pleased with what I do for you.

Amen.

WHO YOU ARE

> *I am changing your name. It will no longer be Abram; now you will be known as Abraham, for you will be the father of many nations.*
>
> GENESIS 17:5 NLT

God understands who you are. God knows the real you. He sees more in you than you see in yourself. He sees inside the person you seem to be to the depths of who you actually are when you respond to his grace and gifts in your life.

When you know the real you that God knows, your confidence level zooms up the scale. When you see yourself as God does, you recognize what strengths you have and what accomplishments you are capable of. You take the high road in all things because you know that's where you belong. Commonplace and ordinary no longer appeal to you. They are not who you are.

You are more than you think you are. You are who God knows you to be.

The effect of righteousness will be peace [internal and external], and the result of righteousness will be quietness and confident trust forever.

ISAIAH 32:17 AMP

Dear God, give me the ability to see myself as you see me.

Amen.

DON'T MISS IT

People need more than bread for their life;
they must feed on every word of God.

MATTHEW 4:4 NLT

Jenny Lind was a talented opera singer known as the Swedish Nightingale. She per-

formed all over the world and toured the United States in the 1850s under the management of P. T. Barnum. She thrilled thousands.

Surprising everyone, Jenny Lind retired at the pinnacle of her career to live in quiet seclusion with her husband. She never returned to the stage. A friend went to visit her and found Jenny Lind on the beach with a Bible on her lap. Her eyes were focused on a sunset. When asked why she had retired so early, she pointed to the Bible and said, "Because every day made me forget this." Then she pointed to the sunset. "And that."

Nothing in life is as important and precious as your appreciation of God.

The thing you should want
most is God's kingdom and
doing what God wants. Then
all these other things you
need will be given to you.

MATTHEW 6:33 NCV

Dear God, I appreciate the
many and creative ways in
which you are known to me.

Amen.

INSPIRED BY GOD

Now I am putting you in the care of God and the message about his grace. It is able to give you strength, and it will give you the blessings God has for all his holy people.

ACTS 20:32 NCV

Frederick W. Robertson of Brighton was one of the great preachers of any age. A tradesman in Brighton kept a picture of Robertson in the back room of his shop. Whenever the tradesman was tempted to do something wrong in his business or behave in an unsuitable way of any kind, he rushed into the back room and looked a long time at the photograph. What he knew about Robertson motivated him to do what was right.

What you know about God inspires you to live the life he wants you to live. When you meditate on God, you are inspired and encouraged to follow his will and walk in his way.

Those you know who walk with God cast a long and strong shadow over your life.

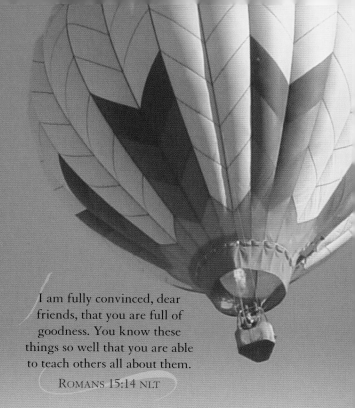

I am fully convinced, dear friends, that you are full of goodness. You know these things so well that you are able to teach others all about them.

ROMANS 15:14 NLT

Dear God, make me a pebble in the water, creating ripples that reach out to others.

Amen.

K KNOW WHAT'S COMING

God raised the Lord from death,
and he will also raise us by his power.
1 CORINTHIANS 6:14 GNT

When you get to know God, you come to trust his power in your life. When disappointment pulls a cloud over your heart, you know God is able to bring you again to a clear and bright day. When you fail at something you were determined to achieve, you know God is able to move you forward in hope and confidence. Whatever happens, you know God is with you to help you.

When you are certain of God's help, you can face anything. When you know God's power is your strength, you can stand anything. You can fall and not despair because you know God will lift you up.

God, who raised Jesus from the dead, brings you the victory of new life every day.

You are from God and have
overcome them, for he who is
in you is greater than he who
is in the world.

1 JOHN 4:4 ESV

Dear God, thank you for coming
to me when I need you most.

Amen.

GLOW AS YOU GO

It came about when Moses was coming down from Mount Sinai . . . that Moses did not know that the skin of his face shone because of his speaking with Him.

EXODUS 34:29 NASB

God's glory shines through you, and you are a joyous reflection of his splendor and character. As Michael Caine said of his profession, "A bad actor is a picture. A good actor is a reflection." You are God's reflection.

Stand outside on a clear night and watch the moon illuminate an entire landscape. By its light you can see all around and know what is there and what isn't. Yet the moon has no light of its own. It reflects the brightness of the sun. It mirrors the light the sun makes.

You reflect the glory that comes from God. He is the source of all light and life.

There in front of his disciples,
Jesus was completely changed.
His face was shining like the
sun, and his clothes became
white as light.

MATTHEW 17:2 CEV

Dear God, put your glory on me
and help me to show it to others.

Amen.

WORSHIP IS RESPONSE

GOD passed in front of him and called out, "GOD, GOD, a God of mercy and grace, endlessly patient—so much love, so deeply true."

EXODUS 34:6 THE MESSAGE

Hearing the word that God had spoken about himself, Moses bowed his head, bent his knee, and worshiped the one who had shown his presence. Your response to God's awesome presence is worship. Worship is the only reasonable response when you begin to know God.

Worship is an offering of your life to God in response to his life in you. When Nehemiah asked Ezra to read holy Scripture, the people responded by bowing low and worshiping God with their faces to the ground. The truth of God in their minds and hearts led them to bow their knees in worship.

Worship is a response to who God is to you and what he does in your life.

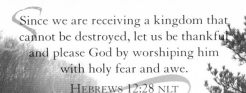

Since we are receiving a kingdom that cannot be destroyed, let us be thankful and please God by worshiping him with holy fear and awe.

HEBREWS 12:28 NLT

Dear God, when I consider all you are to me, I worship and exalt your holy name.

Amen.

STANDING TALL

All the nations—and you made each one—will come and bow down before you, Lord; they will praise your great and holy name.

You can stand tall in the world when you bow low in the presence of God. You can be a giant wherever you are if you are a child before God. Humility is a condition that acknowledges how great God is and how dependent you are on him. You are dependent enough to accept the power and strength he offers. You are needy enough to receive God's resources and gratefully watch him elevate your efforts and endeavors.

Knowing how great God is and giving yourself over to his power bring potency and fervor to the life you live each day. You are more able and more effective when you are in the hands of God. God makes everything you do better. Humility puts both you and God in proper perspective.

Humble yourselves under the mighty hand of God, that He may exalt you at the proper time.

1 PETER 5:6 NASB

Dear God, as the stars fade in brightness when the sun comes out, you exceed all things.

Amen.

BUILD SPIRITUAL MUSCLE

God did not give us a spirit of timidity, but a spirit of power, of love and of self-discipline.

2 TIMOTHY 1:7 NIV

Your time with God is a workout that builds spiritual muscle. As you consistently place yourself in the presence of God, you become spiritually fit. You are dependent on the spiritual enrichment that prayer, worship, and reverence provide. You receive from God nutrients of grace that nourish your heart and your soul.

To function as God designs and desires, take good care of your soul. Understand that you are basically a spiritual person having a brief human experience, not the other way around. Made in God's image, you are more spirit than anything else. Develop your spiritual life through the daily disciplines of prayer, meditation, and Scripture reading.

Keep yourself spiritually fit. Exercise each day in the sanctuary of your soul.

We speak about these things,
not with words taught us by
human wisdom but with
words taught us by the Spirit.
And so we explain spiritual
truths to spiritual people.

1 CORINTHIANS 2:13 NCV

Dear God, my inner life is
the most life I have. Through
your Spirit, I nourish and
nurture this great gift.

Amen.

WHY YOU DO IT

Martha was distracted with all her preparations; and she came up to Him and said, "Lord, do You not care that my sister has left me to do all the serving alone?"

LUKE 10:40 NASB

Jesus came to the Bethany home of Mary, Martha, and Lazarus for dinner. Martha was in charge of preparing the meal, and she wanted everything to be perfect. She spent time deciding what would be on the menu. She made certain she had all the necessary ingredients. She prepared the food with care, concern, and precision. She served it on a table creatively set according to the highest protocol. Imagine her shock when Jesus suggested she'd done it all for the wrong reason.

When you do something for God, remember whom you do it for. Remember why you do it. You do it to honor and glorify God. You do it to make his name known.

Do the work of God for the sake of God.

Everything comes from him;
everything happens through
him; everything ends up in
him. Always glory! Always
praise! Yes. Yes. Yes.

ROMANS 11:36 THE MESSAGE

Dear God, may everything I
do for you be done on behalf
of your glory.

Amen.

LET THEM KNOW

Along the way, he encouraged the believers in all the towns he passed through.

ACTS 20:2 NLT

Perhaps the deepest human need is the need to be appreciated. Love the people God gives you, and let them know you love them.

Affirm who they are. Encourage who they can become. Give them your backing. Be generous with tokens of appreciation. Be slow to correct and quick to praise. Treat people as ends in themselves, not as means to an end.

Make someone's day by sending him or her a little note of appreciation. Call someone on the phone and speak of your affection. Send an e-mail that supports someone. Because of what you say, people feel better about their lives and live more confidently. Your words of encouragement put them on their feet and get them on their way.

In the strength of your affirmation, people become themselves.

Joseph . . . whom the apostles called Barnabas (which means "One who Encourages"), sold a field he owned, brought the money, and turned it over to the apostles.

Acts 4:36–37 GNT

Dear God, lead me to those who need encouragement. When they are down, I will lift them up.

Amen.

*Are you tired? Worn out?
Burned out on religion? Come to
me. Get away with me and you'll
recover your life. I'll show you
how to take a real rest.*

MATTHEW 11:28 THE MESSAGE

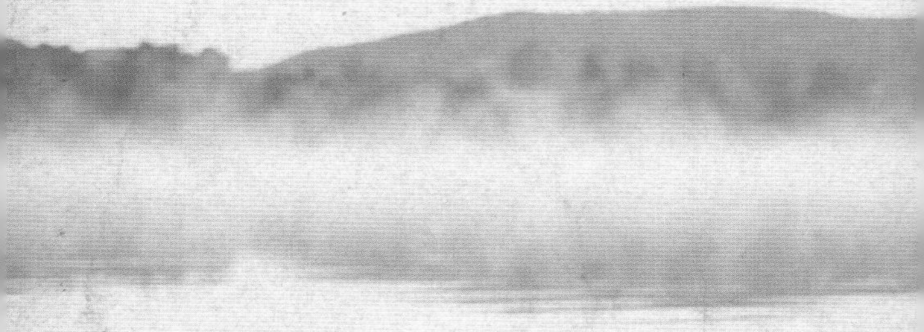

*The LORD is good. When
trouble comes, he is a strong
refuge. And he knows everyone who trusts in him.*

NAHUM 1:7 NLT